Naturopathic Handbook
of
Herbal Formulas

Naturopathic Handbook
of
Herbal Formulas

A Practical and Concise Herb User's Guide

Herbal Research Publications, Inc.
P.O. Box 721
Ayer, Massachusetts 01432
(800) 466-5422

Publisher's Cataloging in Publication

Naturopathic handbook of herbal formulas : a practical and concise herb user's guide. — 4th ed.
p. cm.
ISBN 1-882308-42-5

1. Herbs—Therapeutic use. 2. Naturopathy. I. Title.

RM666.H33S35 1995   615.321
                                          QBI93-503

Fourth Edition
First Printing, 1995
Second Printing, 1996

Printed in the United States of America
3 4 5 6 7 — 99 98 97 96 95

Contents

Fresh Plant Elixirs: Rejuvenative Tonics

Introduction

"In each century since the beginning of the world wonderful things have been discovered. In the last century more amazing things were found out than in any century before. In this new century hundreds of things still more astounding will be brought to light. At first people refuse to believe that a strange new thing can be done, then they begin to hope it can be done, then they see it can be done, then it is done and all the world wonders why it was not done centuries ago."

Frances Hodgson Burnett
from *The Secret Garden*

"Only a new seed will yield a new crop."

Every now and then one comes across opportunities to make decisions which change the course of one's life. During this time, we are witnessing a vast change in society's attitudes and approaches to health and healing. This document is offered to those who recognize the need for this change and for those who are eager to explore the possibilities that it brings.

"The essence of all beings is earth.
The essence of the earth is water.
The essence of water is plants.
The essence of plants is the human being."

Upanishads

Balance in Nature
A Holistic Perspective on the Use of Medicinal Plants

Modern medicine is just now on the verge of discovering a unified field that is the deepest level of nature. Ancient cultures have been aware of this dynamic field for thousands of years. It is considered to be the unexpressed wellspring of intelligence within nature that nourishes and fortifies the infinite diversity expressed in life.

All the laws of nature are contained within this unified field in their seed form. As these impulses of nature flower from their seed form, the intelligence or "mind" of nature becomes expressed in the growth and evolution of every living structure. The life cycle of every plant is governed by these fundamental forces of nature, which have been identified by ancient systems of medicine as earth, air, fire, and water. These building blocks of nature have been recognized respectively by modern chemistry as carbon, oxygen, nitrogen, and hydrogen.

It is through the influence and interaction of these "building blocks" with the plant, that the unexpressed pure intelligence of nature is actually metabolized by the tissues and cells of the plant. The mechanics of this are nothing short of amazing. When a seed changes from its dormant phase to its growth phase, the organizing power of nature within the seed structures the correct balance of earth, air, fire, and water, and orchestrates every phase of development of the plant. Through the process of natural selection the plant organizes the various elemental substances in the soil as well as the elemental values or building blocks of nature into its structure. This is the organizing power of nature at work.

When the human physiology metabolizes a plant remedy, it actually metabolizes the organizing power of nature which the plant has transmuted into material form. In this simple way, the human physiology responds to and is governed by the physiology of nature, resulting in the harmonizing of the body and mind of human life with the "body" and "mind" of nature. The specific value of intelligence and order that is expressed in the cells of the plant is metabolized and expressed into the cells of the physiology.

The Value of Plants in Health and Healing

The metabolism of nature's intelligence by human physiology takes place on the level of the neuroreceptors, which serve as a link between the body and the environment. The human body has a multitude of neuroreceptors that respond to complementary biological substances found in nature. Medicinal plants are capable of targeting specific receptors within the body. In this way, the health and balance of the body is restored by the chemistry and organizing power of the plant. Through the plant's influence, we can greatly enhance our ability to "stitch together" the diverse fabrics of our physiology into a more unified whole.

Plants and Holistic Medicine
Whole Plant Extracts vs. Standardized Extracts vs. Common Drugs

Every culture has a history of using plants for healing. At the turn of the century, pharmaceutical practices provided techniques for "standardizing" and "purifying" medicines by isolating active constituents from plants. In today's allopathic medicine, most remedies are synthetic preparations devoid of any life-promoting vital energies. Thus we have witnessed the crude side effects which common drugs have on the physiology.

Traditional herbal medicine has revealed a deep wisdom that modern medicine is just beginning to appreciate. In today's herbal pharmaceutical practices it is well known that every plant requires specific extraction methods to yield the strongest and most vital remedy. For example, some plants are best prepared by boiling for several hours, while others are best prepared by infusing into cold water. Some plants require fermentation, while others need acidifying. Some are best extracted in oil, while others are best extracted in pure grain alcohol. Traditional practices and modern research guide us in the proper methods of preparing plant remedies. The art of preparing a plant remedy lies in knowing about and working with the "mind" and the "body" of the plant to bring forth its healing virtues.

Common drugs and standardized herbal remedies that utilize only limited constituents of a plant do not have the holistic effect within the body that whole plant extracts do. Some standardized herbal preparations favor one active constituent of a plant. Common drugs provide a chemical similar to an active constituent. Both can have strong effects but always at the expense of the whole. In contrast, whole plant extracts, artfully and scientifically prepared, provide the most complete range of the plant's chemistry and synergy and therefore exercise the most holistic influence on the physiology. A standardized extract should always contain the whole plant constituents and not just the active ingredient. Care should also be taken that the extracts are not prepared with any harsh chemicals or solvents, such as acetone or hexane.

The Value of Freshness in Medicinal Plant Preparations

Herbal preparations are only as vital as the plants used to prepare the remedy. An effective herbal extract should capture the essence of nature's vitality and resemble the plant in taste, smell, and color.

In order to achieve these results, fresh living plants used for extraction are best. When a plant is still fresh and succulent, its cells are naturally swollen and most capable of releasing their therapeutic qualities into the extraction menstruum. This is especially true when using plants that rely on volatile oils for their effectiveness. Volatile oils are aromatic and susceptible to depletion when exposed to drying, storage, heat, or light. A good fresh-plant extract of peppermint, for example, should have that rich flavor, taste, and smell which one experiences when chewing a fresh peppermint leaf.

In many cases the degree to which plants are dried proportionally depletes the active, volatile constituents of the plant. Fresh plants are also rich in enzymes which may catalyze the therapeutic constituents of the plant, enabling them to be most holistic in their action upon the body.

There are, however, some exceptions to this principle of freshness. Plants that have very strong organic fixed principles, resins, gums, and seeds, as well as plants that are cathartic in their action, must be dried before extraction. In the case of cathartic plants, drying and aging the plant renders the activity less irritating. In many cases the properties of herbs are altered by drying the plant. One good example is ginger root. In its fresh state, ginger root is warming and diffusive, rather gentle in its action. In its dry state, ginger root is hot and direct, very strong in its action.

Perhaps the best approach to take in preparing herbal extracts is one that enables the extract to mirror the fresh plant as closely as possible. With correct extraction methods, fresh plant extracts appear to accomplish this goal most successfully.

Extraction Techniques
Defining the Terms Used

In herbal pharmacy there are many methods of preparing herbal extracts. Below are definitions of the terms used in the common preparations of herbal remedies. (Please note: These are very condensed descriptions.)

Tinctures

An alcoholic or hydro-alcoholic preparation providing a dry herb strength ratio of 1:5. Thus, tinctures represent an herb strength of one part herb for every five parts extract.

Liquid Extracts

An alcoholic or hydro-alcoholic preparation generally providing a dry or fresh herb strength ratio of 1:2. Liquid extracts are fully saturated preparations representing an herb strength of one part herb for every two parts extract.

U.S. Pharmacopoeia Fluid Extracts

An alcoholic or hydro-alcoholic preparation providing a dry herb strength ratio of 1:1. This means U.S. Pharmacopoeia Fluid Extracts represent a dry herb strength of one part herb for every part extract. In order to accomplish this concentration, special extraction methods and equipment are necessary involving heat and vacuum.

Fresh Plant Fluid Extracts

An alcoholic or hydro-alcoholic preparation providing a fresh herb strength ratio of 1:1. Fresh Plant Fluid Extracts provide one part herb by weight for every part menstruum by volume. Thus Fresh Plant Fluid Extracts utilize a weight/volume ratio which takes into account the moisture content within the fresh plant.

Solid Extracts

An evaporated U.S. Pharmacopoeia Fluid Extract concentrated by evaporation or vacuum extraction to a dry herb ratio of 4:1. This represents four parts herb for every part of extract.

Powdered Extracts

A powdered version of a U.S. Pharmacopoeia Fluid Extract or Solid Extract. These extracts are prepared by evaporation methods to remove all liquids. The concentration ratio of powdered extracts may vary ranging from 1:1 to 10:1 or stronger.

Standardized Extracts

A powdered or liquid extract prepared by methods described above. However, these extracts represent a significantly higher "standardized" level of the major active constituent within the herb. Some standardized extracts are "standardized" by identifying an active constituent and guaranteeing a consistent level of the constituent in the preparation. In this case, no alteration of the ratio of constituents within the plant takes place.

A Comment on Herbal Usage

When using herbs, it is wise to determine whether the compound is to be used therapeutically or tonically. If an herb is to be used therapeutically, it is best to use it for a short period of time (1 to 4 weeks) at the appropriate time of day or evening. Some herbs are more effective when taken during the morning hours (i.e., Greater Celandine) while others are more effective when taken during the evening hours (i.e., Milk Thistle Seed).

If an herb or compound is to be used tonically (to alter a deep imbalance), it is best to use for a long period of time (4 to 6 months or longer). For example, Hawthorn Berry, a wonderful cardiovascular tonic, exerts its influence best when used 6 to 12 months consecutively.

Invariably, one should apply the simple principle of "rest/ activity" when using herbs. A general recommendation would be to use herbs six days on and one day off, six weeks on and one week off, six months on and one month off. Each period of rest from herbal usage allows the effects of the herbs to become integrated into the physiology.

A very simple analogy will illustrate this. When one wants to dye a white cloth blue, one dips the cloth in dye and then sets it in the sun to dry. When dry, it is noticeable that some of the color has been lost, yet some remains. Again the cloth is dipped in the dye and set back in the sun to dry. Some color again is lost, but more remains. The alternation of this process of "rest and activity" enables the color to become steadfast. Likewise, periodic days of "rest" from herbal remedies enable the physiology to integrate the effects of the herbal compounds and make those effects permanent.

This principle of rest and activity is a fundamental law of nature which governs all growth and evolution of life. Incorporating this principle into herbal usage greatly simplifies, yet profoundly strengthens, the process of using herbs in the healing arts.

Compounding Herbs
Creating Synergy

Herbal compounding is the selection of two or more therapeutic plants combined together to benefit the physiology. The ancient herbal systems of Chinese Medicine and Indian Ayurvedic Medicine provide illustrations of this in their materia medicas.

Medicinal plants are compounded to: increase therapeutic effectiveness; alter individual actions of herbs; and minimize or negate any toxic side effects of unusually strong herbs. In Chinese Medicine, herbs are compounded to enhance the individual constituents. There is always a primary herb within the compound that represents the thrust of the formula. The other herbs enhance, assist, or direct the primary herb in its action. In Ayurvedic Medicine, herbs are often compounded with metals and minerals to bring out the positive effects and neutralize the toxic effects of stronger herbs.

Herbal compounding invariably creates a synergy which enables the formula to function most effectively. This art and science has been practiced for over 5,000 years and today forms the core of clinical herbalism.

Dosage Definitions

In the pages that follow, dosage intervals are noted in Latin abbreviations. The equivalent English intervals are as follows:

q.d.	once a day
b.i.d.	two times a day
t.i.d.	three times a day
q.i.d.	four times a day
gtt	drops

Dispensatory Guide to the Use of Herbal Compounds
A Therapeutic Reference

This Dispensatory Guide is intended to assist in the professional use of botanical formulas. It is not intended to replace physicians' healthcare. It is written for educational purposes only. If a medical condition is present, it would be wise to seek the counsel of a professionally-trained and licensed naturopathic physician.

Compounded Artemisia/Quassia
An Anti-Parasitic Formula

CONTENTS
Fresh Wormword Herb (*Artemisia annua*), Quassia Bark (*Picaraena excelsa*), Fresh Black Walnut Hulls (*Juglans nigra*), Neem Leaves (*Azadirachta indica*), Bilva Herb (*Aegle marmelos*), *Embelia ribes*, *Eclipta alba*, *Phyllanthus amarus*, Gentian Root (*Gentiana lutea*), Fresh Ginger Root (*Zingiber officinalis*)

THERAPEUTIC ACTIONS
This compound contains bitter principles which activate secretions of the digestive and alimentary canals. The vermifuge and vermicide activity is strong, acting upon a wide range of worms, amoebas, and parasites.

INDICATIONS
This compound is indicated whenever there may be a suspicion of pinworms, ringworms, round worms, tapeworms,

microbial growth, and parasitic activity. Also this compound can be used to address fungal and yeast growth, both internally as well as locally.

USES/DOSAGE

Take 30-40 drops of this compound 3 to 5 times daily in a small amount of warm water. While using this compound it would be wise to avoid the foods which parasites and worms thrive upon: sugar, refined carbohydrates, processed foods, etc. Drink plenty of warm water throughout the day to accelerate the effects of these herbs. Use this compound no longer than 3 weeks at a time.

CONTRAINDICATIONS/CAUTIONS

Do not use this compound during pregnancy or whenever there may be chronic illness present. Modify dosage accordingly for children.

Compounded Astragalus
A Deep Immune-Enhancing Formula

CONTENTS

Chinese Astragalus Root (*Astragalus membranaceus*), Chinese Schizandra Berry (*Schizandra chinensis*), Chinese Ligustrum Berry (*Ligustrum lucidum*)

THERAPEUTIC ACTIONS

This compound targets the body's deepest line of defense. The herbs bring support to all deep immune functions and activate cellular immunity. This compound may be used therapeutically for chronic conditions as well as tonically for deep immune support.

INDICATIONS

Use these herbs when there is chronic immune deficiency or breakdown of the deep immune functions. Use as an adjunct in the treatment of cancer, AIDS, arthritis, lupus, blood disorders, anemia, amenorrhea, Epstein-Barr Virus (EBV). This compound may also be used when there are recurring cold/flu infections which prevail chronically throughout the winter.

COMPLEMENTARY COMPOUNDS

This compound is compatible with other deep plant adaptogens such as Siberian Ginseng and Compounded Rejuvenative Elixir, as well as Compounded Elixir of Siberian Ginseng and Compounded Reishi/Bupleurum.

USES/DOSAGE

Take 30-40 drops of the compound 3 to 5 times daily in a small amount of warm water. Best results are achieved when used for 4 to 6 months or longer. If chronic cold/flu syndrome is present, do not use this compound during acute cold symptoms.

Compounded Bloodroot/Celandine
An Anti Retro-Viral Formula

CONTENTS

Fresh Bloodroot (*Sanguinaria canadensis*), Fresh Celandine Flowering Tops and Roots (*Chelidonium major*), Prickly Ash Bark (*Xanthoxylum clava-herculis*)

THERAPEUTIC ACTIONS

This compound contains potent alkaloids which target the category of viruses known as retro-viruses. These alkaloids exhibit an inhibitory effort upon the reverse transcriptase enzyme which is the enzyme used by retro-viruses to transcribe the viral genetics into the genetics of the human cell. This compound may be an effective tool in the management of retro-viral infections.

INDICATIONS

This compound is used to manage the progression of retro-viruses at the genetic level of the cell. Retro-viruses include HIV, Epstein-Barr Virus (EBV), mononucleosis, and herpes.

COMPLEMENTARY COMPOUNDS

Add to the above compound Fresh Thuja Extract (for 2 weeks only), Compounded Astragalus, Fresh St. Johnswort Extract, Licorice Root Solid Extract, Compounded Lomatium, and Reishi Mushroom Extract.

USES/DOSAGE

Take 10-15 drops of this compound 3 to 4 times daily in a small amount of warm water. Use for 2 weeks, then discontinue use for 2 weeks. If opportunistic infection is present use the complementary herbs cited below.

CONTRAINDICATIONS/CAUTIONS

Do not use this compound during pregnancy. Do not take this compound for longer than 2 weeks consecutively as the alkaloids may cause liver distress.

Compounded Bugleweed/Motherwort
An Over-Active Thyroid Formula

CONTENTS

Fresh Bugleweed Herb (*Lycopus virginica*), Fresh Motherwort Flowering Tops (*Leonurus cardiaca*), Fresh Lemon Balm Leaves (*Melissa officinalis*)

THERAPEUTIC ACTIONS

This compound targets the thyroid stimulating hormone and may normalize a hyperactive thyroid condition.

INDICATIONS

This compound is used for an over-active thyroid associated with symptoms of excessive metabolism, cardiac distress/-cardiac neuroses, palpitations, fatigue, anxiety, weight loss.

USES/DOSAGE

Take 30-40 drops of this compound 3 to 4 times daily in a small amount of warm water. This compound may be taken for 3 to 4 months then discontinued for 1 month.

CONTRAINDICATIONS/CAUTIONS

Hyperactive thyroid condition may indicate a more serious health imbalance. It is important to consult your healthcare provider if there is any question regarding the nature of this imbalance.

Compounded Camellia/Curcuma
An Herbal Antioxidant Formula

CONTENTS

Green Tea (*Camellia sinensis*), Turmeric Root (*Curcuma longa*), Ginkgo Leaf (*Ginkgo biloba*), Licorice Root (*Glycyrrhiza glabra*), Siberian Ginseng Root (*Eleutherococcus senticosus*), Rosemary Leaf (*Rosemarinus officinalis*), Thyme Leaf (*Thymus vulgaris*), Schizandra Berry (*Schizandra chinensis*), Ginger Root (*Zingiber officinalis*)

THERAPEUTIC ACTIONS

This herbal compound serves as a powerful antioxidant scavenging free radical molecules. Free radicals are formed through many metabolic processes and are associated with over 80% of all chronic illness.

INDICATIONS

The herbs in the compound enhance tissue integrity and strengthen the immune process and thus may be used as a preventative measure for 4 to 6 months annually.

COMPLEMENTARY COMPOUNDS

This compound will stand alone in its application but its effects will be enhanced with the use of Compounded *Coleus forskohlii*.

USES/DOSAGE

Add 30-40 drops of extract to a small amount of warm water and take 3 to 4 times daily between meals. Use only as directed.

CONTRAINDICATIONS/CAUTIONS

Do not use these herbs during pregnancy and lactation.

Compounded Coleus forskohlii
An Intracellular cAMP Formula

CONTENTS

Coleus forskohlii, Chinese Bupleurum Root (*Bupleurum falcatum*), Feverfew Leaf and Flower (*Tanacetum parthenium*), Chinese Skullcap Root (*Scutellaria biacalensis*), Jujube Dates (*Ziziphus jujube*), Licorice Root (*Glycyrrhiza glabra*), Ginger Root (*Zingiber officinalis*)

THERAPEUTIC ACTIONS

The herbs in this compound raise intracellular levels of cAMP. cAMP acts as the secondary messenger within the cell carrying out the role of hormones at the receptor sites to insure that hormones accomplish what they are intended to accomplish. In a certain way, cAMP coordinates the intelligence within the body to ensure that all the parts are fully connected to the whole. cAMP is regarded as a cell regulating compound. Once it is formed within the cell, it activates many enzymes involved in diverse cellular functions.

INDICATIONS

Indicated for the following imbalances: asthma, allergic conditions, elevated blood pressure, cardiac insufficiency, angina, congestive heart failure, psoriasis, hypothyroidism, malabsorbtion in digestive disorders, depression, immune system enhancement, excessive weight gain, and prevention of cancer metastasis.

COMPLEMENTARY COMPOUNDS

This compound will stand alone in its application but it may also be used with any other herbal therapy and to enhance the effectiveness of the treatment.

USES/DOSAGE

Add 40-60 drops of extract to a small amount of warm water and take 4 times daily between meals. Use only as directed.

CONTRAINDICATIONS/CAUTIONS

Do not use these herbs during pregnancy and lactation.

Compounded Dandelion/Fennel
A Digestive Cordial

CONTENTS

Fresh Dandelion Root and Leaf (*Taraxacum officinalis*), Fennel Seed (*Foeniculum vulgare*), Gentian Root (*Gentiana leutea*), Fresh Peppermint Leaf (*Mentha piperita*), Licorice

Root (*Glycyrrhiza glabra*), Fresh Ginger Root (*Zingiber officinalis*)

THERAPEUTIC ACTIONS

This compound contains bitter principles that activate digestive secretions and enrich enzymatic activity upon food metabolism. Also, carminative herbs provide a soothing influence that dispels wind and gases accumulated in the stomach and intestines. This compound may also be used as a tonic for restoring digestive functions.

INDICATIONS

This compound is used for abnormal digestive secretions, hypochloridia, gall bladder and liver congestion and stagnation, bloating and abdominal distention, excessive gas in the intestinal tract, abnormal appetite, excess heat in the liver and blood. The pleasant taste of this compound makes it an enjoyable cordial to take after meals to lighten the influences of heavy foods and post-digestive heaviness.

USES/DOSAGE

Take 30-40 drops of this compound 3 times daily in a small amount of warm water after meals. These herbs may be taken for 4 to 6 months consecutively.

Compounded Devil's Claw/Chaparral
An Anti-Arthritic Formula

CONTENTS

Devil's Claw Root (*Harpagophytum procumbens*), Chaparral Leaf (*Larrea tridentata*), Fresh Compounded Echinacea

(*Echinacea spp.*), Fresh Burdock Root and Seed (*Arctium lappa*), Fresh Black Cohosh Root (*Cimicifuga racemosa*), Licorice Root (*Glycyrrhiza glabra*), Prickly Ash Bark (*Xanthoxylum clava-herculis*)

THERAPEUTIC ACTIONS

This compound contains antiinflammatory, antioxidant, and immune-enhancing compounds which act to relieve the inflammatory activities associated with arthritic rheumatism.

INDICATIONS

As this is a compound that alleviates inflammation of tissues and muscles, specific indications for this compound include muscular rheumatism and degenerative arthritis associated with deficient immune functions. This compound may also be used for tissue injury manifesting acute inflammations.

COMPLEMENTARY COMPOUNDS

As a broad and comprehensive approach to arthritis, it is suggested that this compound be used with Compounded Red Clover and Compounded Juniper Berry for general tissue and blood alteration. For additional support, herbal salicylates found in Willow Bark and Meadowsweet are very useful as well as Compounded Turmeric/Catechu which contains natural flavonoids to promote tissue integrity and greater antioxidant activity.

USES/DOSAGE

Take 30-40 drops 3 to 4 times daily in a small amount of warm water between meals. This compound and its complementary compounds should be taken for 6 months or longer to effect a good result.

Compounded Devil's Club
A Blood Sugar Balancing Formula

CONTENTS

Fresh Devil's Club Root Bark (*Oplopanax horridum*), Jambul Seed (*Syzygium jambolanum*), Fresh Dandelion Root and Leaf (*Taraxacum officinalis*), Fresh Uva Ursi Leaf (*Arctostaphylos uva ursi*), Fresh Turmeric Root (*Curcuma longa*)

THERAPEUTIC ACTIONS

This compound acts upon the re-synthesis of glycogen, facilitates in the repair of the islets of Langerhans of the pancreas, and promotes better production and utilization of insulin. Since this is a balancing compound, its action is to normalize and restore integrity of the organs and glands associated with carbohydrate and sugar metabolism.

INDICATIONS

These herbs are indicated in both hyper- and hypoglycemia. Use as an adjunct to the daily diet for promoting a greater balance of glucose metabolism within the body.

COMPLEMENTARY COMPOUNDS

In both hyper- and hypoglycemia it is useful to use this compound along with Compounded Elixir of Bitters, which promotes a greater balance to the digestive functions.

USES/DOSAGE

Take 30-40 drops of extract and add to a small amount of warm water. Take shortly before meals, 3 times daily. Continue to use this compound for 3 to 4 months.

CONTRAINDICATIONS/CAUTIONS

This compound should not be taken during pregnancy and should not necessarily be considered a substitute for insulin therapy.

Compounded Dong Quai
A Female Hormone Balancing Formula

CONTENTS

Chinese Dong Quai Root (*Angelica sinensis*), Helonias Root (*Chamaelirium luteum*), Fresh Black Cohosh Root (*Cimicifuga racemosa*), Fresh Squaw Vine (*Mitchella repens*), Fresh Saw Palmetto Berry (*Serenoa repens*), Licorice Root (*Glycyrrhiza glabra*), Fresh Ginger Root (*Zingiber officinalis*)

THERAPEUTIC ACTIONS

This compound targets the ovaries and uterus and lends both a nourishing and tonifying influence to these organs. The herbs exert a balancing effect upon the hormonal functions pertaining to the monthly cycle.

INDICATIONS

As a hormonal balancing compound, dysfunctions relating to hormonal imbalances are addressed with this compound. It is effective in correcting the problems of amenorrhea (absence of or delayed menses), dysmenorrhea (painful menstruation), menorrhagia (excessive menstrual bleeding), and metrorrhagia (excessive uterine bleeding). This compound may also be used to address painful ovulation or ovarian pain, as well as an adjunct therapy in the treatment of endometriosis. Also useful for pelvic atony and prolapsed pelvic organs.

COMPLEMENTARY COMPOUNDS

This compound is synergistic with Compounded Elixir of Vitex and can be used by alternately taking Compounded Dong Quai during the follicular phase (day 1-14) of the cycle and Compounded Elixir of Vitex during the luteal phase (day 14-28) of the cycle.

USES/DOSAGE

Take 30-40 drops 3 times daily in a small amount of warm

water between meals. Take at least 4 to 6 months for corrective therapy or as a tonic for the entire reproductive system.

SPECIFIC DIFFERENTIATIONS

For dysmenorrhea use with Compounded Feverfew/Jamaican Dogwood. For menorrhagia use with extracts of Yarrow, Shepherd's Purse, and Goldenseal.

Compounded Echinacea
An Anti-Viral and Secretory Immune Formula

CONTENTS

Fresh *Echinacea angustifolia* Root, Fresh *Echinacea purpurea* Root, Fresh *Echinacea purpurea* Flowering Heads, Ripe *Echinacea purpurea* Seed

THERAPEUTIC ACTIONS

This compound targets the secretory immune system (lymphatic system, skin, and mucous membranes) and activates cellular immunity when the cellular integrity is threatened by viral attack. This compound also contains antiinflammatory activity, interferon-like activity, and promotes the production of fibroblasts for wound healing.

INDICATIONS

Echinacea is used most effectively at the onset of secretory viral infections and used in large doses. Specific indications include: sinus, nasal, ear, and throat infections; respiratory tract infections; lymphatic infections; lymphatic swelling; kidney, bladder, and urinary tract infections; ovarian and prostate infections. Other indications for its use include inflammatory arthritis, toxemia of the blood, wounds, and cancers of the secretory tissues. Specifically indicated for the common cold and flu-type viral infections.

COMPLEMENTARY COMPOUNDS

Echinacea may be used compatibly in the treatment of secretory immune conditions with diaphoretic herbs such as Yarrow, Elder Flowers, Peppermint, Ginger, Sage, and Boneset. Other compatible herbs include secretory immune modulators such as Prickly Ash Bark and Spilanthes.

USES/DOSAGE

At the onset of viral infection, add 2-3 teaspoons of Echinacea extract to a small amount of warm water and take as an initial dose. Then follow with subsequent doses of 1-2 teaspoons of Echinacea extract every 2 hours and take for up to 5 days. Children's dose should be modified to 5 drops of extract for every year of age until the adult dose is reached.

Compounded Echinacea/Goldenseal
An Anti-Viral, Anti-Bacterial, Antibiotic Formula

CONTENTS

Fresh *Echinacea spp.*, Fresh Goldenseal Root (*Hydrastis canadensis*), Fresh Oregon Grape Root (*Berberis aquifolium*), Fresh Barberry Root Bark (*Berberis vulgaris*), Fresh St. Johnswort Flowering Buds (*Hypericum perforatum*), Propolis (Bee-harvested Tree Resin)

THERAPEUTIC ACTIONS

This compound contains active alkaloids which act as strong natural antibiotics effective in the treatment of a broad spectrum of bacterial conditions. Microbials which this compound addresses directly include *Staph. spp.*, *Strep. spp.*, *Chlamydia spp.*, *E. coli*, Salmonella, Giardia, Trichomonas, and Candida yeast. The anti-viral properties of this compound address a broad spectrum of viral conditions including secretory viruses and retro-viruses.

INDICATIONS

This compound is indicated for the above cited microbials and viruses. At the onset of viral infection it is recommended in frequent and large doses. It is also indicated in the treatment of the common cold and flu viruses and for infections of the lymphatic system. It may also be used externally as a wash for wounds, cuts, and abrasions as well as for insect bites and bee stings.

COMPLEMENTARY COMPOUNDS

For chronic immune imbalances use with deeper-acting immune enhancers such as Compounded Astragalus, Siberian Ginseng, and Siberian Ginseng Tonic.

USES/DOSAGE

At the onset of viral and bacterial infections, take an initial dose of 2-3 teaspoons of extract in a small amount of warm water. Follow with subsequent doses of 1-2 teaspoons in warm water every 2 hours for a maximum of 5 days.

CONTRAINDICATIONS/CAUTIONS

This product should not be used during pregnancy. Prolonged and large doses of Goldenseal may disturb the balance of micro-flora in the gut and the intestines.

Compounded Echinacea/Red Root
A Blood and Lymphatic Alterative Formula

CONTENTS

Fresh *Echinacea spp.*, Fresh Red Root (*Ceanothus americanus*), Fresh Baptisia Root (*Baptisia tinctoria*), Fresh Thuja Leaf

(*Thuja occidentalis*), Fresh Stillingia Root (*Stillingia sylvatica*), Fresh Blue Flag Root (*Iris versicolor*), Prickly Ash Bark (*Xanthoxylum clava-herculus*)

THERAPEUTIC ACTIONS

The herbs within this compound act as blood and lymphatic alteratives and bring about distinct and definite changes in metabolism, repairing catabolic tissue and waste. This compound also augments the body's natural defense mechanisms by activating natural immune responses.

INDICATIONS

These herbs are indicated for conditions associated with a build-up of catabolic wastes in the tissues. Specifically indicated for cancers, tumor growths, incipient cancers, blood dyscrasias, lymphatic engorgement, cysts, fluid cysts, ovarian cysts, endometriosis, cervical dysplasia, and skin ulcerations. Also indicated for those conditions which are associated with a breakdown of the auto immune system.

COMPLEMENTARY COMPOUNDS

Compounded Echinacea/Goldenseal.

USES/DOSAGE

Take 20-40 drops of extract in a small amount of warm water 3 to 5 times daily between meals. Continue using for 2 to 3 months if necessary.

CONTRAINDICATIONS/CAUTIONS

Do not use this compound during pregnancy. If pathology is present, this compound should not replace medical or alternative medical care.

Compounded Eyebright/Bayberry
Hay Fever, Allergy, Sinus Formula

CONTENTS

Fresh Eyebright Herb (*Euphrasia officinalis*), Fresh Bayberry Root (*Myrica cerifera*), Fresh Goldenseal Root (*Hydrastis canadensis*), Fresh Calamus Root (*Acorus calamus*), Fresh Stinging Nettle Leaf (*Urtica dioica*)

THERAPEUTIC ACTIONS

This compound acts to constrict, condense, and contract the swollen mucous membranes associated with hay fevers and allergies. The astringent and antiinflammatory actions bring tone and firmness to soggy membranes. Also, antibacterial activity enables this formula to check infections associated with the sinus and nasal cavity.

INDICATIONS

This compound should be used for the symptomatic relief of hay fever, allergies, and excessive mucous congestion of the sinus, nasal, ear, and throat. Also specifically indicated for sinus infections associated with excessive catarrhal exudations.

COMPLEMENTARY COMPOUNDS

If sinus infection is present, use compatibly with Compounded Echinacea/Goldenseal.

USES/DOSAGE

Take 30-40 drops of this compound added to a small amount of warm water and take 3 to 5 times daily until symptoms are relieved.

CONTRAINDICATIONS/CAUTIONS

Do not use this compound if excessive dryness of the mucous tissue is already present. Do not use this compound during pregnancy. This compound is designed for short term use only. Use only until symptoms disappear.

Compounded Fennel/Wild Yam
A Gallstone, Fatty Digestion Formula

CONTENTS

Fennel Seed (*Foeniculum vulgare*), Fresh Wild Yam Root (*Dioscorea villosa*), Mayapple Root (*Podophyllum peltatum*), Fresh Dandelion Root and Leaf (*Taraxacum officinalis*), Fresh Celandine Root and Tops (*Chelidonium major*), Fresh California Poppy (*Eschscholzia californica*), Peppermint Oil

THERAPEUTIC ACTIONS

This compound contains principles which have choleretic and spasmolytic properties that promote the release and the flow of congested bile through the gall system, and that relax the muscles and membranes to alleviate spastic cramps associated with gall bladder colic.

INDICATIONS

This compound is indicated for the relief of gall bladder congestion or obstructed gall ducts associated with gall bladder colic, incipient gall stones, and bile stagnation. Individuals who have difficulty digesting fatty and unctuous foods are benefited greatly with this compound.

COMPLEMENTARY COMPOUNDS

The use of Compounded Elixir of Bitters will greatly enhance the actions of this compound.

USES/DOSAGE

Take 30-40 drops of this compound 3 to 4 times daily in a small amount of warm water either before or after meals.

CONTRAINDICATIONS/CAUTIONS

Do not use this compound during pregnancy. This compound must be used with great care if gall stones are present. Please consult your healthcare provider if a medical condition is present.

Compounded Feverfew/ Jamaican Dogwood
A Headache, Migraine, Anti-Pain Formula

CONTENTS

Fresh Feverfew Flowering Herb (*Tanacetum parthenium*), Jamaican Dogwood Bark (*Piscidia erythrina*), Fresh Black Haw Root and Tree Bark (*Viburnum prunifolium*), Fresh St. Johnswort Flower Buds (*Hypericum perforatum*), Fresh Butterbur Root (*Petasites frigida*), Meadowsweet Herb (*Filipendula ulmaria*), Fresh Willow Bark (*Salix spp.*), Fresh Ginger Root (*Zingiber officinalis*)

THERAPEUTIC ACTIONS

The herbs in this compound act as an anodyne (pain relieving), and an antispasmodic. Active principles in these herbs address pain and spasms in all parts of the body.

INDICATIONS

This compound may be used for the relief of pain due to headaches (both tension and migraine headaches), dysmenorrhea (painful menstruation), muscle spasms, muscle/skeletal injuries resulting in pain, intestinal spasms, and painful conditions in the body resulting from chronic arthritis and rheumatism.

COMPLEMENTARY COMPOUNDS

For tension headaches, use with Compounded Elixir of Passionflower. For dysmenorrhea, use with Compounded Elixir of Vitex. For muscle/skeletal injuries, use with Compounded Skullcap/St. Johnswort.

USES/DOSAGE

For the relief of migraine and tension headaches, it is best to start treatment at the conceptual stage of the headache. Administer 1 teaspoon in a small amount of warm water as an initial dose and follow with subsequent doses of 40-60 drops every 30 to 60 minutes until pain is relieved. It is wise to rest during this administration time to facilitate the actions of the herbs. For dysmenorrhea and other acute pain, take 40-60 drops of extract in a small amount of warm water every 1 to 2 hours until pain subsides.

Compounded Fraxinus/Ceanothus
A Uterine Fibroid and Cyst Corrective Formula

CONTENTS

Fresh Mountain Ash Bark (*Fraxinus americanus*), Fresh Red Root (*Ceanothus americanus*), Fresh Life Root (*Senecio aureus*), Mayapple Root (*Podophyllum peltatum*), Fresh Helonias Root (*Chamaelirium luteum*), Fresh Goldenseal Root (*Hydrastis canadensis*), Lobelia Herb and Seed (*Lobelia inflata*), Fresh Ginger Root (*Zingiber officinalis*)

THERAPEUTIC ACTIONS

The herbs in this compound act to remove catabolic wastes from the pelvic cavity, and from uterine and ovarian tissues. These herbs accelerate metabolism and lymph drainage and promote the sloughing-off of wasted tissues.

INDICATIONS

This compound is indicated for the treatment of uterine fibroids, ovarian cysts, and endometriosis, as well as uterine atony, prolapsed pelvic organ, and stagnation of the pelvic viscera.

COMPLEMENTARY COMPOUNDS

For the treatment of uterine fibroids, ovarian cysts, and endometriosis, this compound should be used with Compounded Scudder's Alterative, Compounded Echinacea/Red Root, and Compounded Gelsemium/Phytolacca.* If tissue tension is present in the uterine region, use with Black Cohosh Root as well.

USES/DOSAGE

Use 40-60 drops of this extract in a small amount of warm water and take 3 to 4 times daily for up to 3 to 4 months.

CONTRAINDICATIONS/CAUTIONS

Do not use this compound during pregnancy. *Use only under direct physician's care as the asterisk compound cited above may be toxic if not used properly.

Compounded Garcinia
A Lipolytic, Thermogenic (Weight Loss) Formula

CONTENTS

Green Tea (*Camellia sinensis*), Garcinia-Malabar Tamarind (*Garcinia cambogia*), Coleus Forskohlii Root (*Coleus forskohlii*), Elderberry (*Sambucus canadensis*), Gymnema Leaf (*Gymnema sylvestre*), Bladderwrack Fronds (*Fucus vesiculosis*), Licorice Root (*Glycyrrhiza glabra*), Jujube Dates (*Ziziphus jujube*), Turmeric Root (*Curcuma longa*), Fresh Ginger Root (*Zingiber officinalis*)

THERAPEUTIC ACTIONS

This compound stimulates the process of thermogenesis (the body's production of heat) and thus aids in the capacity to burn calories. It promotes the regulation of appetite thereby regulating the amount and type of food eaten. It also regulates the conversion of carbohydrates to fat which inevitably contributes to the inhibition of lipolysis, the storage of fat particularly at adipose sites. Other therapeutic actions include the inhibition of the uptake of norepinephrine at the alpha 2 receptor sites within the fat cell (alpha 2 uptake of norepinephrine encourages the fat cells to store fat). It stimulates the production of glycogen in the liver which may result in increased energy levels. It also stimulates the production of intracellular cAMP which carries out the influence of the hormone norepinephrine at the beta receptor sites within the fat cell and encourages the process of lipolysis.

INDICATIONS

For stimulation of weight loss and breaking up of stored adipose fat in the thighs, hips, and buttocks.

COMPLEMENTARY COMPOUNDS

This compound may be combined compatibly with Compounded *Coleus forskohlii*.

USES/DOSAGE

Add 40-60 drops of extract to a small amount of warm water and take 3 times daily between meals. Use only as directed.

CONTRAINDICATIONS/CAUTIONS

Do not use these herbs during pregnancy and lactation.

Compounded Gelsemium/Phytolacca
An Ovarian Cyst Formula

CONTENTS

Fresh Gelsemium Root (*Gelsemium sempervirens*), Fresh Poke Root (*Phytolacca americana*) Fresh Aconite (*Aconitum napellus*), Bryonia Root (*Bryonia dioica*)

THERAPEUTIC ACTIONS

The herbs in this compound are considered to be very strong and potentially toxic if misused. They act to dislodge and slough off catabolic waste tissue and promote the drainage of lymphatic fluids from areas affected by the buildup of wastes.

INDICATIONS

This compound is used specifically for the treatment of ovarian cysts and endometriosis. Other uses include severe, irritating, explosive cough and pain associated with tension and tenderness.

USES/DOSAGE

Take 5-8 drops of the compound in a small amount of warm water 2 to 3 times daily for up to 2 weeks. Use only under the care of a licensed naturopathic physician.

CONTRAINDICATIONS/CAUTIONS

Do not use this compound during pregnancy. Do not use with children. This compound may be toxic if used incorrectly.

Compounded Ginseng/Schizandra
An Adrenal, Adaptogenic Formula

CONTENTS

Siberian Ginseng Root (*Eleutherococcus senticossus*), Chinese Schizandra Berry (*Schizandra chinensis*), Damiana Leaf (*Turnera diffusa*), Cola Nut (*Cola nitida*), Fresh Wild Oats (*Avena sativa*), Licorice Root (*Glycyrrhiza glabra*), Fresh Skullcap Herb (*Scutellaria lateriflora*), Prickly Ash Bark (*Xanthoxylum clava-herculis*)

THERAPEUTIC ACTIONS

The herbs in this compound act to restore integrity to the adrenal glands and promote a greater sense of energy and stamina. The adaptogenic properties of these herbs help to build up the body's response to stress. These herbs are also nutritive and tonic to the adrenal glands as well as to nerve cells and tissues.

INDICATIONS

This compound is indicated as an adjunct therapy in the treatment of Addison's Disease (an adrenal deficient disorder). Also specifically indicated for those exhibiting low adrenal function which manifests into low vitality, anemia, low blood pressure, anxiety, physical strain and pressure, and low and depleted energy. As an adaptogen, this compound is very useful for those who are constantly exposed to stressful environments or situations, overwork, excess strain to mind and body, and those involved in weight management and body building programs.

COMPLEMENTARY COMPOUNDS

Use this compound with Siberian Ginseng Tonic, Compounded Smilax/Damiana, or Compounded Elixir of Eleutherox whenever the indications call for any of these compounds.

USES/DOSAGE

Take 30-40 drops of the extract 3 to 4 times daily in a small amount of warm water between meals. Use for 3 to 4 months consecutively for best results.

CONTRAINDICATIONS/CAUTIONS

Do not use this compound during pregnancy. Do not use this compound if there are conditions present associated with hyper-adrenalism.

Compounded Wild Ginseng
An Energy, Anti-Stress, Adaptogenic Formula

CONTENTS

Wild Siberian Ginseng Root (*Eleutherococcus senticosus*), Fresh Wild American Ginseng Root (*Panax quinquifolium*)

THERAPEUTIC ACTIONS

This compound is a classic adaptogenic formula which helps the body adapt to stressful environments and situations more efficiently. The eleutherosides and ginsenosides in this compound have a positive influence upon all major organs and glands, improving the vitality and stamina of the entire psychophysiological system.

INDICATIONS

This compound may be used as a tonic to improve stamina, endurance, energy, and vitality. Specifically indicated where the adrenals are exhausted and the endocrine functions are at a low ebb. Use as a restorative and energizing tonic when stress levels are high.

COMPLEMENTARY COMPOUNDS

To improve energy and vitality, this compound may be used

with Compounded Rejuvenative Elixir and Siberian Ginseng Tonic. When there is mental stress it may be used with Compounded Gotu Kola and Ginkgo extracts.

USES/DOSAGE

Take 10-20 drops of this compound in a small amount of warm water 3 times daily. Best results are achieved if taken for 3 to 4 months consecutively.

CONTRAINDICATIONS/CAUTIONS

Do not take this compound during pregnancy. If cardiac conditions are present, this compound should only be used under care by a naturopathic physician.

Compounded Glyconda Cordial
An Herbal Antacid and Heartburn Remedy

CONTENTS

Turkey Rhubarb Root (*Rheum palmatum*), Fresh Goldenseal Root (*Hydrastis canadensis*), Cinnamon Bark (*Cinnamomum zeylanicum*), Peppermint Essential Oil, Potassium Bicarbonate, Vegetable Glycerine

THERAPEUTIC ACTIONS

This compound targets the upper gastric system and is traditionally used as an herbal alternative to antacids. It has alterative effects on the upper gastrointestinal tract and is useful for both diarrhea and constipation. This pleasant-tasting formula may be combined with bad tasting remedies for administration to children.

INDICATIONS

Use this compound as an alternative to Tums or Rolaids whenever acid indigestion is present. Especially effective for gastritis, heartburn, indigestion, belching, and a feeling of heaviness in the esophagus and stomach.

USES/DOSAGE

Take 40-60 drops in a small amount of warm water or soda water after meals or whenever acid indigestion is present.

Compounded Gotu Kola
A Memory and Mental Adaptogen Formula

CONTENTS

Fresh Gotu Kola Leaf and Root (*Centella asiatica*), Russian Siberian Ginseng (*Eleutherococcus senticosus*), Fresh Ginkgo Leaf (*Ginkgo biloba*), Fresh Wild Oats (*Avena sativa*), Chinese Fo-Ti (He Shou Wu; *Polygonum multiflorum*), Fresh Peppermint Leaf (*Mentha piperita*), Rosemary Leaf (*Rosmarinus officinalis*)

THERAPEUTIC ACTIONS

The herbs in this compound have antioxidant properties which slow down mental aging. Specific actions include improvement to cerebral circulation, peripheral circulation, blood and oxygen supply to the brain, as well as action to reduce the impact which stress has upon the brain and nervous system. Folklore suggests that many of the herbs in this compound directly retard aging of brain and nerve cells.

INDICATIONS

This compound is indicated for short term memory loss, Alzheimer's disease, mental stress and fatigue, impaired peripheral circulation, mental chatter, lack of mental clarity, nervous exhaustion, low adaptive response, and a negative response to stress in general. Use as a general restorative tonic to improve the vitality of the functions of the brain and nerve cells.

COMPLEMENTARY COMPOUNDS

This compound may be used compatibly with Siberian Ginseng Tonic, Compounded Rejuvenative Elixir, and Compounded Elixir of Passionflower.

USES/DOSAGE

Take 30-40 drops of this compound 3 to 4 times daily in a small amount of warm water between meals. Best results are achieved if used for 3 to 4 months consecutively.

CONTRAINDICATIONS/CAUTIONS

This compound should not be used during pregnancy.

Compounded Grindelia/Camellia
An Anti-Asthmatic Formula

CONTENTS

Grindelia Floral Buds (*Grindelia robusta*), Green Tea (*Camellia sinensis*), Licorice Root (*Glycyrrhiza glabra*), Rose Hips Solid Extract (*Rosa rugosa*), Lobelia Herb and Seed (*Lobelia inflata*), Chinese Ephedra (Ma Huang; *Ephedra sinica*), Ginger Root (*Zingiber officinalis*)

THERAPEUTIC ACTIONS

This compound relaxes bronchial smooth muscles and promotes a bronchial/pulmonary dilation which enables a greater flow of oxygen into respiratory apparatus. It also influences sympathomimetic neurofunction (vagus nerve). It also provides necessary adrenal support promoting the secretion of antiinflammatory corticosteroids from the adrenal glands which counteract mediators of inflammation produced through mast cell degranulation.

INDICATIONS

This compound is especially suited for prophylactic use for asthmatics and will aid in reducing the frequency and intensity of asthmatic onsets.

COMPLEMENTARY COMPOUNDS

This compound may be combined compatibly with Compounded *Coleus forskohlii*.

USES/DOSAGE

Add 40-60 drops of extract to a small amount of warm water and take 4 times daily between meals. Use only as directed.

CONTRAINDICATIONS/CAUTIONS

Do not use these herbs during pregnancy and lactation.

Compounded Hawthorn
A Cardiovascular and Connective Tissue Formula

CONTENTS

Hawthorn Berry Solid Extract, Fresh Hawthorn Leaf and Flower (*Crataegus oxyacantha*)

THERAPEUTIC ACTIONS

This compound contains two groups of active flavonoids which exert their actions upon the heart/cardiovascular system and a second group upon the connective tissue. This compound is regarded as a cardiovascular tonic, bringing micro-nutrition and microchemistry to the heart and surrounding arteries and capillaries. It is a true restorative to the cardiovascular system. The connective tissue flavonoids act to reinforce the collagen tissue with cross fibers which strengthen this tissue and promote more vitality to this component of the immune system.

INDICATIONS

This compound is used for rhythmical disturbances of the heart (palpitations, arrhythmias, and tachycardia). Also specifically indicated for myocardial degeneration and acute myocardial insufficiency, cardiac weakness after infections, mitral valve prolapse, elevated cholesterol, hypertension, hypotension, and fatty degeneration of the heart. Other uses include connective tissue support in the treatment of spinal subluxations, inability to hold spinal adjustments, hernias, hemorrhoids, varicosities, prolapsed organs, collagen deficient disorders, and other disorders of the connective tissue.

COMPLEMENTARY COMPOUNDS

This compound may be used effectively with Hawthorn Berry Solid Extract.

USES/DOSAGE

Add 40-60 drops of extract to a small amount of warm water and take 3 to 5 times daily between meals. Best results are achieved if taken over a 6 to 12 month period consecutively.

CONTRAINDICATIONS/CAUTIONS

Do not discontinue the use of this compound abruptly.

Compounded Hoxsey/Red Clover
A Blood and Liver Alterative Formula

CONTENTS

Fresh Red Clover Blossoms (*Trifolium pratense*), Buckthorn Bark (*Rhamnus cathartica*), Fresh Barberry Root Bark

(*Berberis vulgaris*), Fresh Burdock Root (*Arctium lappa*), Fresh Stillingia Root (*Stillingia sylvatica*), Fresh Poke Root (*Phytolacca americana*), Cascara Sagrada Bark (*Rhamnus purshiana*), Licorice Root (*Glycyrrhiza glabra*), Prickly Ash Bark (*Xanthoxylum clava-herculis*). Note: The species of Cascara mentioned in the original Hoxsey formula was thought to be Cascara Amarga (*Sweetia panamensis*), not Cascara Sagrada. Cascara Sagrada is offered as an analog.

THERAPEUTIC ACTIONS

The herbs in this compound are considered to be classic alteratives which alter catabolic tissues in the body and bring about a tissue change where old, diseased tissue is replaced with healthy, new, more vital tissue. Traditionally these herbs were known as blood purifiers. They act to enhance metabolic functions and promote greater drainage and elimination through the eliminative organs.

INDICATIONS

This compound is indicated for the breakdown and removal of metabolic wastes from the body. Specifically indicated for lymphatic engorgement, tumors, incipient cancers, glandular obstructions, and other chronic disorders. This compound provides antiseptic, anti-tumor, and antioxidant activity. It normalizes blood imbalances and activates the clearing and defense mechanisms of the liver.

COMPLEMENTARY COMPOUNDS

This compound should be used most effectively with Compounded Juniper Berry and plenty of warm water throughout the day.

USES/DOSAGE

Add 30-40 drops of extract to a small amount of warm water and take 3 to 5 times daily. Best results are achieved if used for 3 to 4 months consecutively.

CONTRAINDICATIONS/CAUTIONS

Do not use this compound during pregnancy.

Compounded Juniper Berry
A Urinary Diuretic Formula

CONTENTS

Fresh Juniper Berry (*Juniperis communus*), Fresh Spring Horsetail (*Equisetum arvense*), Fresh Corn Silk (*Zea mays*), Fresh Goldenrod Flowering Tops (*Solidago odora*), Fresh Cleavers Herb (*Galium aparine*), Fresh Marshmallow Root (*Althaea officinalis*)

THERAPEUTIC ACTIONS

This compound contains diuretic, antiseptic, and emollient principles which act to gently stimulate renal excretions, disinfect the urinary tract, and soothe irritated urinary membranes. This compound also functions as a restorative tonic to the entire urinary system.

Our kidneys consume much energy in their efforts to remove metabolic wastes from the circulation. Periodic herbal renal support reduces the stress which accumulates throughout the renal system. In this formula, there are several cleansing herbs which have as their primary function to gently stimulate renal excretions causing toxins circulating throughout the blood and lymph to be carried out of the system. Toxins such as calculi, which build in the joints and tissues and which can cause edema and cystitis; impurities in circulation arising from digestive errors; and sediments and gravel which settle in the urinary system causing lumbar pain, painful urination, incontinence, etc.; all these are gradually corrected with the use of this herbal blend. As an adjunct in the Internal Cleansing

Program, Compounded Juniper Berry mildly stimulates the kidneys enabling better renal excretion to take place.

INDICATIONS

This compound is indicated in the treatment of dropsy from renal suppression, cystic catarrh, renal congestion, enuresis, renal obstructions (gravel, bladder stones, calculi), scalding micturition, irritable bladder, cystitis, nephritis, and inability to urinate freely. This compound stimulates the removal of catabolic wastes from the tissues and encourages elimination via the kidneys.

COMPLEMENTARY COMPOUNDS

In alterative therapeutic "blood cleansing," use with Compounded Red Clover and plenty of warm water.

USES/DOSAGE

Add 30-40 drops of extract to a small amount of warm water and take 3 to 5 times daily between meals. Drink plenty of warm water between doses.

CONTRAINDICATIONS/CAUTIONS

Do not use this compound during pregnancy.

Compounded Kava Kava/St. Johnswort
An Anti-Depressant Formula

CONTENTS

Kava Kava Root (*Piper methysticum*), St. Johnswort Floral Buds (*Hypericum perforatum*), Passionflower (*Passiflora incarnata*), Gotu Kola Leaf and Root (*Centella asiatica*),

Schizandra Berry (*Schizandra chinensis*), Siberian Ginseng Root (*Eleutherococcus senticosus*), Wild Oat Seed (*Avena sativa*), Stinging Nettle Seed (*Urtica dioica*), Calamus Root (*Acorus calamus*), Prickly Ash Bark (*Xanthoxylum clava-herculis*)

THERAPEUTIC ACTIONS

Inhibits monoamine oxidase (prevents oxidative deamination of brain amines such as seratonin, melatonin, dopamine, epinephrine, and norepinephrine), provides adrenal support and restoration, strengthens nerve integrity, and promotes general adaptive integrity. Also increases nerve impulse transmitters within the brain which maintain emotional stability and promote a general feeling of balance and happiness.

INDICATIONS

This compound may be used for individuals currently using anti-depression medication and is indicated for mild to moderate depression, anxious depression, fears, anxiety disorders, and emotional imbalances caused by imbalances in adrenergic transmission.

COMPLEMENTARY COMPOUNDS

This compound may be combined compatibly with Compounded *Coleus forskohlii*.

USES/DOSAGE

Add 40-60 drops of extract to a small amount of warm water and take 4 times daily between meals. Best results are achieved if used for 3-4 months consecutively. Use only as directed.

CONTRAINDICATIONS/CAUTIONS

Do not use these herbs during pregnancy and lactation.

Compounded Linden/Crataegus
A Hypertension Formula

CONTENTS

Fresh Linden Flowers (*Tilia spp.*), Compounded Fresh Hawthorn (*Crataegus oxyacantha*), Fresh Mistletoe (*Viscum flavescens*), Fresh Valerian Root (*Valeriana officinalis*)

THERAPEUTIC ACTIONS

The herbs in this compound exert a hypotensive influence and in time will exhibit an anti-arteriosclerotic influence through the absorption of arterial plaque from the walls of the arteries leading to and from the heart.

INDICATIONS

Use this compound in the treatment of essential hypertension, high blood pressure, vascular fragility, and cardiac distress. May also be useful with associated conditions such as arteriosclerosis and high cholesterol.

COMPLEMENTARY COMPOUNDS

To the above compound add Compounded Hawthorn and Dandelion Root and Leaf to accentuate the effect of the compound. If under the care of a fully licensed naturopathic physician, Rauwolfia Root may also be used (with great caution).

USES/DOSAGE

Add 30-40 drops of extract to a small amount of warm water and take 3 to 4 times daily between meals. Continue to use for 3 to 4 months for best results.

CONTRAINDICATIONS/CAUTIONS

Do not use this compound during pregnancy.

Compounded Lobelia/Calamus
A Stop-Smoking Formula

CONTENTS

Fresh Lobelia Herb and Seed (*Lobelia inflata*), Fresh Calamus Root (*Acorus calamus*), Fresh Wild Oat Seed (*Avena sativa*), Fresh St. Johnswort Flower Buds (*Hypericum perforatum*), Fresh Licorice Root (*Glycyrrhiza glabra*), Fresh Passionflower Herb (*Passiflora incarnata*)

THERAPEUTIC ACTIONS

The active principle of this compound, lobeline, is an alkaloid extracted from the Lobelia plant. This alkaloid greatly reduces the desire to ingest nicotine, as the body recognizes the two chemicals in a similar way. Also the adjunct herbs in this compound promote the detoxification of nicotine residues and promote the restoration of the nerve cells and nerve tissues which may have been damaged due to prolonged cigarette smoking.

INDICATIONS

This compound is indicated for individuals who wish to break their smoking habit and at the same time clear out residues left from smoking while restoring important neurological and adrenal functions.

COMPLEMENTARY COMPOUNDS

To assist in the repair of the nervous system, use Compounded Elixir of Passionflower and Compounded Calcium Elixir for 3 to 4 months.

USES/DOSAGE

Add 20-30 drops of extract to a small amount of warm water and take 3 to 4 times daily or more frequently between meals. Continue for 3 to 4 months for best results.

CONTRAINDICATIONS/CAUTIONS

Do not use this compound during pregnancy. If vomiting occurs due to the emetic property of Lobelia, reduce the dose to half the suggested dose.

Compounded Lomatium
An Anti-Viral Formula

CONTENTS

Fresh Lomatium Root (*Lomatium dissectum*), Fresh Echinacea (*Echinacea spp.*), Fresh Spilanthes Flowering Herb and Root (*Spilanthes acmella*), Fresh St. Johnswort Flowering Buds (*Hypericum perforatum*), Chinese Skullcap Root (*Scutellaria baicalensis*), Chinese Schizandra Berry (*Schizandra chinensis*), Licorice Root (*Glycyrrhiza glabra*), Essential Oil of Cinnamon

THERAPEUTIC ACTIONS

This compound contains strong anti-viral activity and immune-enhancing properties. Many of the herbs in this compound target cellular immunity and liver functions and act to protect the healthy cells from viral infection, as well as promote a better flow of the vital force through the liver system.

INDICATIONS

Specifically indicated in the treatment of chronic viral infection including Epstein-Barr Virus (EBV), hepatitis, shingles, mononucleosis, and other liver viruses. This compound is also indicated as an adjunct in the treatment of Candida yeast overgrowth and fungal infections as well as herpes infections.

COMPLEMENTARY COMPOUNDS

Compounded Echinacea/Goldenseal may be used with the

above compound during acute infections. For deeper immune support when there is chronic infection, use with Compounded Astragalus. If there is fungal and yeast overgrowth, use with Compounded Elixir of Bitters and Compounded Spilanthes.

USES/DOSAGE

Add 30-40 drops of extract to a small amount of warm water and take 3 to 4 times daily between meals. For best results, take 3 to 4 months consecutively.

CONTRAINDICATIONS/CAUTIONS

Do not use this compound during pregnancy. If a skin rash appears from the use of this compound, discontinue its use. Although this happens infrequently, it indicates a high sensitivity to Lomatium Root and this compound should not be used.

Compounded Melissa
A Children's Hyperactivity Formula

CONTENTS

Fresh Lemon Balm (*Melissa officinalis*), Fresh Chamomile Flowers (*Matricaria chamomilla*), Fresh Passionflower (*Passiflora incarnata*), Fresh Skullcap Herb (*Scutellaria lateriflora*), Fresh Wild Oat Seed (*Avena sativa*), Fresh Gotu Kola Glycerite (*Centella asiatica*), Mineral salts extracted from Kelp, Irish Moss, and other seaweeds

THERAPEUTIC ACTIONS

This compound contains nervine and tonic principles which both relax and restore to balance the functions of the brain and nerve cells. Although this compound does not promote sleepiness or lethargy, it quiets down the agitation and over excitability of the nervous system.

INDICATIONS

This compound is very effective in the treatment of children's hyperactivity and anxiety-tetanic patterns, nervous sensitivity and excitability, and attention deficit disorders. As a restorative tonic, this compound may be used during the daytime to reduce hyperactivity and at bedtime to promote deep and efficient sleep. This compound may also be used by adults who exhibit similar difficulties as well as excessive mental chatter and nervous and mental irritation.

COMPLEMENTARY COMPOUNDS

To improve the effectiveness of this compound, Compounded Elixir of Passionflower and California Poppy may be used as well as Glycine amino acid.

USES/DOSAGE

Add 20-30 drops of extract to a small amount of warm water and take 3 to 4 times daily between meals. For best results, take this compound for 3 to 4 months or longer.

Compounded Milk Thistle/Yellow Dock
A Skin Corrective Formula

CONTENTS

Milk Thistle Seed (*Silybum marianum*), Fresh Yellow Dock Root (*Rumex crispus*), Fresh Burdock Root (*Arctium lappa*), Fresh Echinacea (*Echinacea spp.*), Sarsaparilla Root (*Smilax officinalis*), Fresh Oregon Grape Root (*Berberis aquifolium*)

THERAPEUTIC ACTIONS

This compound targets the organs of metabolism and corrects

metabolic errors which are responsible for the manifestation of skin disorders. Yellow Dock addresses skin disorders associated with improper fatty metabolism; Burdock Root addresses skin disorders associated with impure blood; Echinacea addresses skin disorders associated with bacterial growth; Sarsaparilla Root addresses skin disorders associated with hormonal imbalance; and Milk Thistle Seed and Oregon Grape Root address skin disorders associated with improper liver metabolism.

INDICATIONS

This compound is specifically indicated for a broad spectrum of dermatological conditions including oily acne, cystic acne, hormonal acne, blackheads, pimples, eczema, psoriasis, seborrhea, psoriatic arthritis, and many other skin disturbances. This compound may also be used as a wonderful spring tonic to promote an alteration of catabolic wastes which have built up over the winter. The chemistry and nutrients of the herbs in this compound promote restoration and well-being of the skin as an organ.

COMPLEMENTARY COMPOUNDS

This compound may be used compatibly with Compounded Juniper Berry and plenty of warm water throughout the day.

USES/DOSAGE

Add 30-40 drops of extract to a small amount of warm water and take 3 to 4 times daily. Best results are achieved if taken over 3 to 4 months consecutively.

CONTRAINDICATIONS/CAUTIONS

Do not use this compound during pregnancy.

Compounded Plantain/Buchu
A Urinary Incontinence Formula

CONTENTS

Fresh Plantain Leaf and Corm (*Plantago lanceolata*), African Buchu Leaves (*Barosma betulina*), Fresh Corn Silk (*Zea mays*), Fresh Horsetail Grass (*Equisetum arvense*), Fresh St. Johnswort Flower Buds (*Hypericum perforatum*), Fresh Arnica Flowers (*Arnica latifolia*), Fresh Thuja Leaf (*Thuja occidentalis*)

THERAPEUTIC ACTIONS

The herbs in this compound act to strengthen the musculature and tone the membranes of the urinary system. The soothing and restorative properties of these herbs relieve irritation and weakness of the urinary tract.

INDICATIONS

This compound is specifically indicated for urinary incontinence in both children and adults. Also may be used as a restorative tonic to strengthen the musculature of the pelvic organs.

USES/DOSAGE

Add 20-30 drops of extract to a small amount of warm water and take 3 to 4 times daily for up to 2 to 3 months. Children's dose should be lowered to 5-15 drops 3 to 4 times daily and taken for 1 to 2 months.

CONTRAINDICATIONS/CAUTIONS

This compound should not be taken during pregnancy.

Compounded Psyllium Husks
A Digestive, Internal Cleansing Formula

CONTENTS

Psyllium Husks, Ayurvedic Triphala Powder, Marshmallow Root Powder, Licorice Root Powder, Ginger Root Powder.

ACTIONS AND INDICATIONS

This formulation of herbs works remarkably well to revitalize digestion and improve absorption of food nutrients, while at the same time enhancing the elimination of wastes from the intestinal tract. The herbs in this blend promote a soothing bulk influence to the intestines. Triphala powder, an ancient Ayurvedic herbal blend, helps to enhance the functions of the organs of digestion and assimilation while revitalizing the entire metabolic processes. The effect of this synergistic blend of herbs is to remove putrefactive gases and wastes from the intestinal flora, expel mucous and endogenous toxins from the intestines, and relieve digestive and intestinal distress and irritation. Regular use of the Compounded Psyllium Husk each season promotes digestive and eliminative well-being.

DOSAGE

Use 1 teaspoon in 8-10 ounces of warm water and take 2 times daily. Shake well before using.

Compounded Red Clover
A Blood and Lymphatic Alterative Formula

CONTENTS

Fresh Red Clover Blossoms (*Trifolium pratense*), Fresh Stinging Nettle Leaf (*Urtica dioica*), Fresh Cleavers Herb (*Galium aparine*), Fresh Yellow Dock Root (*Rumex crispus*), Fresh

Burdock Root (*Arctium lappa*), Fresh Yarrow Flowers (*Achillea millefolium*), Fresh Plantain Leaf and Corm (*Plantago lanceolata*), Licorice Root (*Glycyrrhiza glabra*), Prickly Ash Bark (*Xanthoxylum clava-herculis*)

THERAPEUTIC ACTIONS

The herbs in this compound are classic blood and lymphatic alteratives which alter the catabolic tissue conditions and bring about an improved state of well-being through improved metabolism and elimination. These herbs target the organs of metabolism, improving their functions and restoring their vitality by carrying more blood and nutrient supply to the cellular level and promoting greater excretion at the cellular level.

The influence of these herbs gradually alters the composition and constitution of the blood and lymph. This is accomplished through the removal of metabolic wastes which build up in the circulatory fluids and through the gentle nourishing and remineralizing effect that these herbs have upon the blood. Also, wasted tissues and cells are sloughed off and directed to eliminative channels for removal from the body. At the same time, new healthy tissue growth is encouraged with this herbal blend. Excessive impurities in the circulatory fluids are oftentimes the cause of metabolic changes in the body tissue and skin which may eventually give rise to tissue damage and dermatitis conditions such as eczema and psoriasis. Compounded Red Clover cools excess heat in the blood and liver which is associated with these disturbances. Compounded Red Clover is also effective for toxemia, lymph stagnation, lymph edema, swollen lymph glands, etc. Compounded Red Clover and Compounded Juniper Berry work synergistically together to correct blood impurities and remove them through proper eliminative channels.

INDICATIONS

This compound cools excess heat in the blood and liver and may be used specifically in the treatment of cancer, eczema, psoriasis, tumors, cysts, toxemia, lymphedema, swollen and caseated lymph nodes, psoriatic and gouty arthritis, acne, and all skin disturbances. This compound may also be used as a spring tonic to promote detoxification.

COMPLEMENTARY COMPOUNDS

This compound combines well with Compounded Juniper Berry and should be used with plenty of warm water throughout the day. (For specific indications please refer to the Herbal Repertory).

USES/DOSAGE

Add 30-40 drops of extract to a small amount of warm water and take 3 to 4 times daily. Best results are achieved if taken for 2 to 4 months consecutively.

CONTRAINDICATIONS/CAUTIONS

Do not use this compound during pregnancy.

Compounded Reishi/Bupleurum
An Anti Retro-Viral, Immune-Enhancing Formula

CONTENTS

Reishi Mushroom (*Ganoderma lucidum*), Chinese Bupleurum Root (*Bupleurum falcatum*), Astragalus Root (*Astragalus membranaceus*), St. Johnswort Floral Buds (*Hypericum perforatum*), Chinese Skullcap Root (*Scutellaria baicalensis*), Lomatium Root (*Lomatium dissectum*), Red Root (*Ceanothus americana*), Licorice Root (*Glycyrrhiza glabra*), Thuja Leaf (*Thuja occidentalis*), Prickly Ash Bark (*Xanthoxylum clavaherculis*)

THERAPEUTIC ACTIONS

The herbs in this compound stimulate cellular immunity

enabling the immune cells to become more immunologically competent. Research has indicated that these herbs strongly inhibit retro-viruses as well as reverse-transcriptase enzyme. This compound of herbs targets the very deepest level of defense triggering the production of immune cells from the bone marrow and also triggering the process through which those cells are potentiated via the thymus gland.

INDICATIONS

Indicated for the prophylactic treatment of retro-viruses and deep immune system compromise. Also indicated to strengthen and preserve the vital force in healthy individuals.

COMPLEMENTARY COMPOUNDS

This compound may be combined compatibly with Compounded *Coleus forskohlii*, Compounded Astragalus, and Compounded Sheep Sorrel/Burdock.

USES/DOSAGE

Add 40-60 drops of extract to a small amount of warm water and take 4 times daily between meals. Use only as directed.

CONTRAINDICATIONS/CAUTIONS

Do not use these herbs during pregnancy and lactation.

Compounded Robert's Formula
A Digestive Corrective Formula

CONTENTS

Fresh Compounded Echinacea (*Echinacea angustifolia* and *Echinacea purpurea*), Fresh Marshmallow Root (*Althaea officinalis*), Fresh Goldenseal Root (*Hydrastis canadensis*), Fresh Geranium Root (*Geranium maculatum*), Fresh Slippery

Elm Bark (*Ulmus rubra*), Fresh Poke Root (*Phytolacca americana*)

THERAPEUTIC ACTIONS

This compound targets the lining of the gastrointestinal tract and corrects enteric bacterial imbalances and functional disturbances of the entire intestinal tract.

INDICATIONS

Useful in the treatment of gastric ulcers, gastric irritation, irritable bowel syndrome, spastic colon, bacterial imbalances of the colon, toxemia, and digestive metabolic disorders.

COMPLEMENTARY COMPOUNDS

If treating gastric ulcers, this compound is most effective if used with Deglycyrrhizinated Licorice Powder. Also useful to use with Compounded Glyconda Cordial.

USES/DOSAGE

Take 30-50 drops of extract in a small amount of warm water 3 to 4 times daily between meals.

CONTRAINDICATIONS/CAUTIONS

Do not use this compound during pregnancy.

Compounded Saw Palmetto
A Men's Prostate Formula

CONTENTS

Fresh Saw Palmetto Berry (*Serenoa repens*), Fresh Echinacea (*Echinacea spp.*), Fresh Stinging Nettle Root (*Urtica dioica*), Poplar Bark (*Populus tremulodies*), Fresh Pipsissewa Herb (*Chimaphila umbellata*), Fresh Thuja Leaf (*Thuja occidentalis*)

THERAPEUTIC ACTIONS

The herbs in this compound target the prostate gland and surrounding tissues and promote better secretions, better lymphatic drainage, and waste excretions from the genito-urinary system.

INDICATIONS

This compound is indicated in the treatment of benign prostatic hyperplasia (BPH), prostatic infections, prostatitis, gravel, sedimentation, spermatorrhea, difficulty in passing urine freely, nocturnal urination, painful urination.

COMPLEMENTARY COMPOUNDS

For the above-cited conditions, use with Pygeum Bark and Fresh Poke Root Extract as well as Compounded Juniper Berry.

USES/DOSAGE

Add 30-50 drops of extract to a small amount of warm water and take 3 to 4 times daily as a corrective measure. Drink plenty of warm water throughout the day when using this compound.

CONTRAINDICATIONS/CAUTIONS

If prostatic problems are present, please seek professional naturopathic advice.

Compounded Schizandra/Silybum
An Alcohol Recovery Formula

CONTENTS

Schizandra Berry (*Schizandra chinensis*), Milk Thistle Seed (*Silybum marianum*), Wild Oat Seed (*Avena sativa*), Kudzu Root (*Pueraria lobata*), Indian Gooseberry (*Emblica officinalis*), Passionflower (*Passiflora incarnata*), Licorice Root

(*Glycyrrhiza glabra*), Peppermint Leaf (*Mentha piperita*), Ginger Root (*Zingiber officinalis*)

THERAPEUTIC ACTIONS

The herbs in this compound act to restore hepatocyte integrity as well as to protect liver cells from endogenous and exogenous toxins. Alcohol cravings are curbed with the ingestion of this compound. Individuals who have suffered from liver damage caused by excessive ingestion of abusive substances will find that this compound greatly revitalizes the functions of the liver.

INDICATIONS

The herbs in this compound are used for chronic alcohol abuse, to restore damaged liver function, and to curb the craving for alcohol.

COMPLEMENTARY COMPOUNDS

This compound stands alone in its application as a liver restorative after chronic alcohol abuse.

USE/DOSAGE

Add 40-60 drops of extract to a small amount of warm water and take 3 to 4 times daily between meals. Use only as directed.

CONTRAINDICATIONS/CAUTIONS

Do not use these herbs during pregnancy and lactation.

Compounded Scudder's Alterative
A Deep-Tissue Cleansing Formula

CONTENTS

Corydalis Tubers (*Dicentra canadensis*), Fresh Black Alder Bark (*Alnus serrulata*), Mayapple Root (*Podophyllum peltatum*), Figwort Flowering Herb (*Scrophularia nodosa*), Fresh Yellow Dock Root (*Rumex crispus*)

THERAPEUTIC ACTIONS

This excellent alterative compound was originally prepared according to Prof. Scudder's formula (an eclectic medical formula). It acts, as all alteratives do, to replace catabolic tissue with healthy, more vibrant tissue. This is an alterative second to none, working to bring about a repair to the vital force through the removal of obstructing waste material.

INDICATIONS

Specifically indicated in liver and glandular afflictions, skin disorders, lymphatic and blood disorders, tumors, cysts, boils, carbuncles, cancers, endometriosis, and conditions where there is waste build-up and deranged tissue.

COMPLEMENTARY COMPOUNDS

This compound may be used harmoniously with Compounded Juniper Berry and plenty of warm water.

USES/DOSAGE

Add 30-40 drops of extract to a small amount of warm water and take 3 to 4 times daily. Best results are achieved if taken for 2 to 4 months consecutively.

CONTRAINDICATIONS/CAUTIONS

Do not use this compound during pregnancy.

Compounded Sheep Sorrel/Burdock
An Alterative Formula for Degenerative Processes

CONTENTS

Fresh Sheep Sorrel (*Rumex acetosella*), Fresh Burdock Root

(*Arctium lappa*), Fresh Slippery Elm Bark (*Ulmus rubra*), Turkey Rhubarb Root (*Rheum palmatum*)

THERAPEUTIC ACTIONS

This compound is a replication of Renee Caisse's formula used extensively for the treatment of degenerative disorders. It alters the process of waste and nutrition helping to break down catabolic tissue and promote the replacement of wasted tissue with healthy new tissue.

INDICATIONS

Use this compound when there is chronic degenerative illness as a prophylactic treatment. May also be used as another fine alterative to aid in the maintenance of a healthy constitution.

USES/DOSAGE

Take 30-50 drops of extract in a small amount of warm water and take 3 to 4 times daily between meals.

CONTRAINDICATIONS/CAUTIONS

Do not take this compound during pregnancy.

Compounded Skullcap/St. Johnswort
A Nerve, Trauma, and Sleep Formula

CONTENTS

Fresh Skullcap Herb (*Scutellaria lateriflora*), Fresh St. Johnswort Flower Buds (*Hypericum perforatum*), Fresh Calendula Flowers (*Calendula officinalis*), Fresh Chamomile Flowers (*Matricaria chamomilla*), Fresh California Poppy (*Eschscholzia californica*), Fresh Wild Oats (*Avena sativa*), Fresh Valerian Root (*Valeriana officinalis*)

THERAPEUTIC ACTIONS

This compound is a nerve restorative, antispasmodic, and soothing anodyne formula. The specific herbs in this compound repair damaged and irritated nerves, soothe nervous agitation and excitability, and exert a mild sedative action to help promote sleep.

INDICATIONS

This compound is specifically indicated for the treatment of nerve and muscle spasms, nerve trauma, nerve injury, and nervous agitation. As a restorative, it repairs the vital force after injury, trauma, or shock. It is specifically useful in the treatment of anxiety, insomnia, hyper-excitability, tension, nerve exhaustion, and nerve disturbances. This compound can also be used as an anti-viral agent both topically and internally for the treatment of shingles and herpes.

COMPLEMENTARY COMPOUNDS

The actions of the herbs in this compound are enhanced with the use of Compounded Elixir of Passionflower.

USES/DOSAGE

Add 30-40 drops of extract to a small amount of warm water and take 3 to 4 times daily between meals.

CONTRAINDICATIONS/CAUTIONS

Do not use this compound during pregnancy.

Compounded Smilax/Damiana
A Male/Female Virility Formula

CONTENTS

Sarsaparilla Root (*Smilax officinalis*), Damiana Herb (*Turnera diffusa*), Fresh Wild American Ginseng Root (*Panax quinquifolium*), Ashwagandha (Winter Cherry; *Withania somnifera*), Shatavari Root (Asparagus Root; *Asparagus racemosus*), Fresh Wild Oat Seed (*Avena sativa*), Licorice Root (*Glycyrrhiza glabra*), Hawthorn Berry (*Crataegus oxyacantha*), Prickly Ash Bark (*Xanthoxylum clava-herculis*)

THERAPEUTIC ACTIONS

This compound contains natural phytosterols and other natural hormonal-like compounds which target the same receptors as endogenous hormones. The herbs bring a natural enlivening influence throughout the body and mind. The restorative and tonic actions of the herbs enable more stamina, vitality, endurance, and virility to be enjoyed.

INDICATIONS

This compound is specifically indicated for individuals desiring greater stamina and virility. It is useful as an adjunct to body-building programs and programs designed to enhance athletic performance. It is also useful when there is deficiency and anemia associated with a weak constitution.

COMPLEMENTARY COMPOUNDS

This compound may be used compatibly with Siberian Ginseng Tonic and Compounded Ginseng/Schizandra.

USES/DOSAGE

Add 30-40 drops of extract to a small amount of warm water and take 3 to 4 times daily between meals. Best results are achieved if taken over a 3 to 4 month period.

CONTRAINDICATIONS/CAUTIONS

Do not take this compound during pregnancy.

Compounded Spilanthes
An Anti-Yeast and Anti-Fungal Formula

CONTENTS

Fresh Spilanthes Flowering Tops and Root (*Spilanthes acmella*), Fresh Oregon Grape Root (*Berberis aquifolium*), Fresh Juniper Berry (*Juniperus communis*), Usnea Lichen (*Usnea spp.*), Myrrh Gum (*Commiphora mukul*)

THERAPEUTIC ACTIONS

The herbs in this compound contain natural anti-fungal, anti-bacterial, and anti-yeast properties.

INDICATIONS

This compound is specifically indicated in the treatment of Candida yeast overgrowth, vaginal infections, fungal infections (finger and toenail fungus), athlete's foot, and ringworm. This compound may also be used as an adjunct in the treatment of Epstein-Barr Virus (EBV).

COMPLEMENTARY COMPOUNDS

The use of Compounded Elixir of Bitters is very effective as an adjunct to overcoming yeast overgrowth.

USES/DOSAGE

Add 30-40 drops of extract to a small amount of warm water and take 3 to 4 times daily between meals. Best results are achieved if taken over a period of 3 to 4 months.

CONTRAINDICATIONS/CAUTIONS

Do not take this compound during pregnancy.

Compounded Turmeric/Catechu
An Immediate-Type Hypersensitivity, Allergy, and Antiinflammatory Formula

CONTENTS

Fresh Turmeric Root (*Curcuma longa*), Black Catechu (*Catechu nigra*), Fresh Grindelia Floral Buds (*Grindelia robusta*), Licorice Root (*Glycyrrhiza glabra*), Rose Hips (*Rosa rugosa*), Chinese Skullcap (*Scutellaria baicalensis*), Fresh Ginkgo Leaf (*Ginkgo biloba*), African Devil's Claw Root (*Harpagophytum procumbens*), Fresh Yarrow Flowers (*Achillea millefolium*), Fresh Lobelia Herb and Seed (*Lobelia inflata*)

THERAPEUTIC ACTIONS

The herbs in this compound contain active constituents which act as antiinflammatory, antihistamine, bronchial dilators, respiratory antispasmodics, and membrane integrity enhancers. Also, these herbs are powerful anti-hepatotoxic in that they protect the liver from circulating antigens/allergens. This compound is formulated to provide adrenal support when epinephrine is needed by the body to compensate for the inflammatory responses generated from the presence of allergens. A specific mode of action of this compound is to stabilize mast cells of the respiratory membranes, mucous membranes, and epidermal skin tissue.

INDICATIONS

This compound is specifically indicated for the treatment of all disorders of immediate-type hypersensitivity including allergies, asthma, urticaria, reactive dermatitis, reactive arthritis, reactive irritable bowel syndrome, anaphylaxis, food sensitivities, sinusitis, and other acute and chronic inflammations.

COMPLEMENTARY COMPOUNDS

As an adjunct to the therapy please refer to other formulas listed in this section as well as in the Herbal Repertory section. Specifically, refer to "Botanical Protocols for Disorders of Immediate Type Hypersensitivity" at the end of this book.

USES/DOSAGE

Add 30-40 drops of extract to a small amount of warm water and take 4 to 5 times daily between meals. Best results are achieved if taken for 3 to 4 months. Drink plenty of warm water while using this compound.

Compounded Usnea/Uva Ursi
A Urinary Tract Antibiotic Formula

CONTENTS

Usnea Lichen (*Usnea spp.*), Fresh Uva Ursi Leaf (*Arctostaphylos uva ursi*), Fresh Pipsissewa Leaf (*Chimaphila umbellata*), Fresh Echinacea (*Echinacea spp.*)

THERAPEUTIC ACTIONS

This compound contains natural antibiotic and antibacterial compounds which target directly the urinary system.

INDICATIONS

This compound is specifically indicated in the treatment of bladder infections, kidney infections, urinary tract infections, and cystitis, as well as nephritis. This preparation may also be used for chronic urinary irritation and chronic bladder irritation.

COMPLEMENTARY COMPOUNDS

Add to the above compound Uva Ursi Solid Extract.

USES/DOSAGE

Add 40-60 drops of extract to a small amount of warm water and take every 1 to 2 hours until symptoms of urinary infections disappear. Use this formula for a maximum of 5 to 7 days only.

CONTRAINDICATIONS/CAUTIONS

Do not use this compound during pregnancy. Use only for a maximum of 5 to 7 days. If symptoms of urinary tract infections are present, please consult your naturopathic physician. Do not use this formula with cranberry juice as the juice will neutralize the actions of the herbs.

Compounded Valerian/Poppy
An Herbal Insomnia Formula

CONTENTS

Valerian (*Valerian officinalis*), Skullcap (*Scutellaria lateriflora*), California Poppy (*Eschscholzia californica*), Kava Kava Root (*Piper methysticum*), Passionflower (*Passiflorus incarnata*), Chamomile (*Matricaria chamomilla*), Mugwort (*Artemisia vulgaris*)

THERAPEUTIC ACTIONS

The therapeutic actions of this compound are sedative, anxiolytic, and nerve restorative. As the sedative herbs target and tonify sleep functions within the body, the restorative herbs, skullcap and passionflower, nourish and revitalize nerve centers and nerve cells.

INDICATIONS

This formula is specifically indicated for insomnia due to

nervous tension, anxiety, or stress. It is recommended that it be used as needed ½ to 1 hour before bedtime.

COMPLEMENTARY COMPOUNDS

This compound may be used compatibly with Compounded Elixir of Passionflower and Compounded Calcium Elixir.

USES/DOSAGE

Add 40-60 drops every 20 minutes beginning one hour before bedtime (for a maximum of three doses).

CONTRAINDICATIONS/CAUTIONS

Do not use this compound during pregnancy and lactation, or while operating machinery or driving, or while participating in activities which require exertion or alertness.

Compounded Vitex/Alfalfa
A Menopausal Corrective Formula

CONTENTS

Chaste Tree Berry (*Vitex agnus-castus*), Alfalfa Leaf (*Medicago sativa*), Night Blooming Cereus (*Cactus grandiflorus*), St. Johnswort Flower Buds (*Hypericum perforatum*), Sage Leaf (*Salvia officinalis*), Fresh Wild Oat Seed (*Avena sativa*), Fresh Motherwort Flowering Tops (*Leonurus cardiaca*), Essential Oil of Lavender

THERAPEUTIC ACTIONS

The herbs in this compound assist in the balancing of the Follicle Stimulating Hormone (FSH) and the Luteinizing Hormone (LH). This compound has a restorative effect upon the corpus luteum and enables the body to maintain a minimal amount of progesterone secretion from the corpus luteum which in turn enables estrogen levels to increase. Also, this compound addresses symptoms which are prevalent during menopause. These symptoms normalize as the hormones become balanced.

INDICATIONS

This compound is specifically indicated for the treatment of hot flashes, night sweats, depression, skin changes and anxiety during menopause, and other changes such as bone loss (osteoporosis) during menopause.

COMPLEMENTARY COMPOUNDS

This compound should be used with Compounded Elixir of Vitex and Alfalfa Solid Extract and Wild Yam Extract as natural substitutes for estrogen replacement therapy.

USES/DOSAGE

Add 30-40 drops of extract to a small amount of warm water and take 3 to 4 times daily between meals. Best results are achieved if taken for 3 to 4 months consecutively.

Compounded Wild Cherry
An Anti-Coughing Formula

CONTENTS

Fresh Wild Cherry Bark (*Prunus serotina*), Fresh Elecampane Root (*Inula helenium*), Yerba Santa Leaf (*Eriodictyon californicum*), Fresh Red Clover Blossoms (*Trifolium pratense*), Licorice Root (*Glycyrrhiza glabra*), Fresh Butterbur Root (*Petasites frigida*)

THERAPEUTIC ACTIONS

This compound contains respiratory antispasmodic principles and soothing emollient principles which target the lungs and respiratory membranes.

INDICATIONS

This compound is used in the treatment of dry, irritative coughs, whooping cough, asthmatic cough, spastic cough, bronchial irritation. It loosens hardened catarrh from the respiratory lining and promotes the expectoration of this catarrh and mucous.

COMPLEMENTARY COMPOUNDS

This compound may be used with any of the following herbs in the treatment of spastic coughs: Lobelia, Grindelia, Marshmallow Root, Comfrey Root, Slippery Elm Bark, Pleurisy Root, and Lungwort Lichen.

USES/DOSAGE

Add 30-50 drops of extract to a small amount of warm water and take 3 to 5 times daily between meals. Use as often as necessary to relieve the symptoms of irritative cough.

Compounded Yucca/Burdock
An Anti-Arthritic, Antiinflammatory Formula

CONTENTS

Fresh Yucca Root (*Yucca spp.*), Fresh Echinacea (*Echinacea spp.*), Fresh Burdock Root and Seed (*Arctium lappa*), Fresh Poke Root (*Phytolacca americana*), Celery Seed (*Apium graveolens*), Bladderwrack Fronds (*Fucus vesiculosus*), Fresh Pipsissewa Herb (*Chimaphilla umbellata*)

THERAPEUTIC ACTIONS

The herbs in this compound have strong antiinflammatory compounds. Specific actions also include diuretic properties as well as properties to alkalize an over-acid body chemistry which is generally associated with arthritis.

INDICATIONS

This compound is indicated for the treatment of gouty arthritis, psoriatic arthritis, articular rheumatism (rheumatism of the small joints), and arthritis associated with a febrile constitution (over-acid body chemistry). The herbs in this compound dislodge acids and crystals in tissues and promote their excretion through the urinary system.

COMPLEMENTARY COMPOUNDS

This compound should be used with Compounded Red Clover and Compounded Juniper Berry to accent the effectiveness of the herbs. Use plenty of warm water when taking this compound.

USES/DOSAGE

Add 30-40 drops of extract to a small amount of warm water and take 3 to 5 times daily between meals. Best results are achieved if taken over 3 to 4 months consecutively.

CONTRAINDICATIONS/CAUTIONS

Do not use this compound during pregnancy.

Fresh Plant Elixirs
Rejuvenative Tonics

The compounds listed below are best prepared and used as herbal elixirs. In this fashion they are truly tonic to the physiology and rejuvenate the deep body tissues of the systems which they target. One of the key features of these Elixir Compounds is the addition of several species of sea vegetation and marine algae to the formulation. The micro-nutrition contained within the seaweeds provides a rich source of minerals and trace minerals which target the same receptors the primary herbs in the compound target. In this way, the tissues and cells of the body not only receive the influence of the plants, but also the influence of the micro-nutrition. Thus, the vital force is fortified at the tissue and cellular level. The end result is a very deep restoration and rejuvenation of the organs and systems which the Elixir Compounds target.

Compounded Rejuvenative Elixir
A Tonic to Renew the Vitality of the Body and Mind

CONTENTS

Amalaki (Indian Gooseberry), Siberian Ginseng, Fresh Gotu Kola Leaf and Root, Fresh Ginkgo Leaf, Fresh Ligustrum Berry, Prickly Ash Bark, Hawthorn Berry Solid Extract, Rose Hip Solid Extract, Concentrated Apricot and Mulberry Syrup, Custom Extract of Sea Vegetation and Marine Algae, Vegetable Glycerine

ACTIONS AND INDICATIONS

Promotes longevity of body tissues, balances the composition of the blood and lymph and regenerates healthy brain and nerve cells. Supports the immune system and enhances energy and clarity of perception. Use specifically as a tonic to renew the vitality of the body and mind.

DOSAGE

Use 1 teaspoon 3 times daily between meals.

Compounded Vitamin C Elixir
An Organic Plant Source of Vitamin C

CONTENTS

Amalaki (Indian Gooseberry), Rose Hips Solid Extract, Custom Extract of Sea Vegetation and Marine Algae, Sweet Orange Essence, Vegetable Glycerine

ACTIONS AND INDICATIONS

Use as an organic plant source of Vitamin C. Derived from Amalaki fruits growing wild in India, each fruit contains nearly 3,000 mg of organic Vitamin C. The actions of this delicious elixir are to strongly enhance body immune response against colds, flus, and infections, to enhance capillary integrity, to rebuild and maintain body tissues, and to enhance the vitality of every cell.

DOSAGE

Use 1 teaspoon 3 times daily between meals.

Compounded Nutritional Elixir
A Tonic to Invigorate the Blood Chemistry

CONTENTS

Fresh Nettle Leaf, Fresh Wild Oats, Fresh Red Clover Blossoms, Fresh Red Raspberry Leaf, Fresh Yellow Dock Roots, Fresh Gentian Roots, Fresh Elderberries, Amalaki (Indian Gooseberry), Alfalfa Solid Extract, Rose Hips Solid Extract, Hawthorn Berry Solid Extract, Concentrated Syrup of Apricots and Mulberries, Chlorella, Custom Extract of Sea Vegetation and Marine Algae, Vegetable Glycerine

ACTIONS AND INDICATIONS

The rich mineral salts represented in this compounded tonic invigorate the blood chemistry and normalize iron deficiency, enabling more vital oxygen to nourish the brain cells. A specific for anemics or any deficiency or as an alterative to any vitamin/mineral supplement. Can also be used as an energy tonic providing more vitality to body and mind. This compound also facilitates and enhances enzyme activity promoting an increased uptake of nutrition into the cells.

DOSAGE

Use 1 teaspoon 3 times daily between meals.

Compounded Calcium Elixir
A Bone, Flesh, Cartilage, and Connective Tissue Tonic

CONTENTS

Fresh Comfrey Root, Fresh Marshmallow Root, Fresh Black Walnut Leaf and Hulls, Fresh Skullcap Herb, Fresh Mullein Leaf, Fresh St. Johnswort Flower Buds, Fresh White Oak Bark, Fresh Gravel Root, Fresh Horsetail Herb, Hawthorn Berry Solid

Extract, Mineral Ash of Alfalfa Leaf and Nettle Leaf, Concentrated Extract of Sea Vegetation and Marine Algae (especially Kelp and Bladderwrack)

ACTIONS AND INDICATIONS

Use as an agent to facilitate the uptake of calcium salt and to promote the healing of wounds, injuries, broken bones, burns, torn cartilage, torn ligaments, etc. Also very effective in promoting quick recovery after a chronic illness by strengthening the vital force.

DOSAGE

Use 1 teaspoon 3 to 4 times daily when needed. Use for up to 3 months consecutively then discontinue its use for 2 to 3 months.

Compounded Elixir of Passionflower
A Nerve Tonic and Restorative

CONTENTS

Fresh Passionflower, Fresh Skullcap Herb, Fresh Chamomile Flowers, Fresh Hops Strobile, Fresh Wild Oats, Fresh Mugwort Leaf, Fresh Peppermint Leaf, Hawthorn Berry Solid Extract, Concentrated Apricot and Mulberry Syrup, Custom Extract of Sea Vegetation and Marine Algae, Vegetable Glycerine, Peppermint Essence.

ACTIONS AND INDICATIONS

Especially useful in anxiety conditions, hyperactivity, trauma, restlessness, and insomnia. The elixir fortifies the nerve cells with rich trace elements, enhances nerve vitality, relieves tissue tension in the stomach and digestive tract, and encourages a free flow of nerve energy through the physiology. This is not a sedative and can be used during the daytime to counteract anxiety, and at night to facilitate easy sleep.

DOSAGE

Use 1 teaspoon 3 times daily between meals.

Compounded Elixir of Siberian Ginseng
An Adaptogenic Tonic

CONTENTS

Siberian Ginseng Solid Extract, Royal Jelly, Schizandra Berries, Fresh Yellow Dock Root, Fresh Gentian Root, Prickly Ash Bark, Rose Hips Solid Extract, Chlorella, Custom Extract of Sea Vegetation and Marine Algae

ACTIONS AND INDICATIONS

An adaptogenic tonic useful in all deficient constitutions. Useful as an adjunct in building blood and raising the quality of the vital force. Provides increased energy, strength, and clarity. Excellent tonic for rehabilitation and geriatrics. A specific for anemia, deficient menses, physical weakness of long standing nature, and immune deficient syndromes.

DOSAGE

Use ½-1 teaspoon 3 times daily between meals.

Compounded Elixir of Bitters
A Sweet/Bitter Digestive Tonic

CONTENTS

Amalaki (Indian Gooseberry), Fresh Turmeric Root, Mature

Milk Thistle Seed, Fresh Wild Yam Root, Fennel Seed, Cardamon Seed, Fresh Calamus Root, Anise Seed, Bitter Orange Oil, Ginger Root, Custom Extract of Sea Vegetation and Marine Algae

ACTIONS AND INDICATIONS

An extremely valuable aid in revitalizing the digestive functions by enhancing secretions of the liver, pancreas, stomach, and small intestine. This compounded elixir provides rich enzyme catalysts which improve nutrient absorption. This compound also protects the liver from endogenous toxins and normalizes gut and intestinal flora. Other indications include flatulence, constipation, abdominal bloating, digestive distress, and sluggish peristalsis.

Sluggish elimination is often a result of reduced secretions from the digestive organs and small intestine. Excessive refined foods generate stress upon the liver and pancreas and impede the natural metabolic functions. This is one reason why traditionally in almost every culture, herbal bitters are used. Compounded Elixir of Bitters represents a most effective blend of rejuvenative and carminative herbs which mildly stimulate and gently tonify the glands and digestive organs. Primary herbs in this formula are Turmeric Root and Indian Gooseberry. Both are indigenous to India, where they have been used traditionally to strengthen and protect the liver from endogenous toxins. Indian Gooseberry has also been shown to contain enzyme catalysts which improve nutrient absorption from the intestines. The other herbs in the formula work synergistically with these primary herbs to protect the liver from toxic overload, to tonify the liver, gallbladder, and pancreas, and to normalize stomach secretions. The volatile oils found in Fennel Seed, Cardamon Seed, and Anise Seed dispel gases from the stomach and intestines while Turmeric Root and Ginger Root normalize peristalsis and intestinal flora in the stomach and intestines.

DOSAGE
Use ½ teaspoon in warm water 3 times daily before meals.

Compounded Elixir of Vitex
A Female Hormone Corrective Tonic

CONTENTS
Fresh Chaste Tree Berry, Fresh Squaw Vine, Fresh Black Haw Bark, Fresh Butterbur Root, Fresh Mugwort Leaf, Fresh Dandelion Leaf and Root, Usnea Lichen, Rose Hips Solid Extract, Concentrated Mulberry Syrup, Custom Extract of Sea Vegetation and Marine Algae, Vegetable Glycerine

ACTIONS AND INDICATIONS
This compounded elixir corrects imbalances of estrogen metabolism associated with excessive catechol estrogens and elevated inflammatory prostaglandins. Therefore, it is very useful in the treatment of PMS, amenorrhea, dysmenorrhea, endometriosis, and menopausal imbalances.

DOSAGE
Use 1 teaspoon 3 times daily between meals. This compounded elixir must be used for 4 to 6 months consecutively. During the premenstrual phase, dosage may be increased to 1 teaspoon 4 to 5 times daily.

Compounded Elixir of Eleutherox
A Male Revitalizing Tonic

CONTENTS
Siberian Ginseng, Sarsaparilla Root Solid Extract, Fresh Saw

Palmetto Berry, Fresh Ligustrum Berry, Rose Hips Solid Extract, Fresh Dandelion Root and Leaf, Usnea Lichen, Concentrated Mulberry Syrup, Custom Extract of Sea Vegetation and Marine Algae, Vegetable Glycerine

ACTIONS AND INDICATIONS

Useful for athletes during workout phase, for energy enhancement, and increased physical endurance. This compound may provide steroid-like activity, thus its value in athletic training.

DOSAGE

Use 1 teaspoon 3 times daily between meals.

Compounded Vata Tonic
A Vata Type Soothing Elixir

CONTENTS

Gotu Kola Leaf and Root (*Centella asiatica*), Wild Oat Seed (*Avena sativa*), Ashwagandha (*Withania somnifera*), Shatavari (*Asparagus racemosus*), Chinese Fo-Ti (*Polygonum multiflorum*), Licorice Root (*Glycyrrhiza glabra*), Cinnamon Bark (*Cinnamonum zeylanicum*), Ginger Root (*Zingiber officinalis*)

ACTIONS AND INDICATIONS

This soothing compound is formulated to nourish and revitalize the Vata constitution type. The herbs contained within this compound strengthen the vital force and support the nervous system, mental functions, and sleep patterns, and bring greater flexibility to the joints. The Vata predominating constitution requires a greater sense of balance and relaxation within the functions of the nervous system and is in general need of replenishment to the vital energies.

DOSAGE

Take 30-60 drops (½-1 teaspoon) 3 times daily in a small amount of warm water between meals.

CONTRAINDICATIONS/CAUTIONS

Do not use these herbs during pregnancy and lactation.

Compounded Pitta Tonic
A Pitta Type Balancing Elixir

CONTENTS

Turmeric Root (*Curcuma longa*), Indian Gooseberry (*Emblica officinalis*), Milk Thistle Seed (*Silybum marianum*), Schizandra Berry (*Schizandra chinensis*), Licorice Root (*Glycyrrhiza glabra*), Cardamon Seed (*Elettaria cardamomum*), Gentian Root (*Gentiana lutea*), Fennel Seed (*Foeniculum vulgare*)

ACTIONS AND INDICATIONS

This balancing elixir addresses the root cause of many Pitta disturbances – digestive errors. The herbs contained within the compound target the digestive organs and glands, restoring secretions, assimilation, and elimination. The foundation of a strong Pitta constitution is a healthy metabolism and strong digestion. This elixir brings support to this important physiological function and promotes balance within all aspects of the Pitta constitution.

DOSAGE

Take 30-60 drops (½-1 teaspoon) in a small amount of warm water 3 times daily between meals.

CONTRAINDICATIONS/CAUTIONS

Do not use these herbs during pregnancy and lactation.

Compounded Kapha Tonic
A Kapha Type Invigorating Elixir

CONTENTS

Green Tea (*Camellia sinensis*), Elderberry (*Sambucus canadensis*), Cola Nut (*Cola nitida*), Nettle Seed (*Urtica dioica*), Fenugreek Seed (*Trigonella foenum-graecum*), Clove Buds (*Syzygium aromaticum*), Ginger Root (*Zingiber officinalis*)

ACTIONS AND INDICATIONS

This invigorating elixir enlivens the naturally sluggish Kapha constitution as it restores strength and vigor to the metabolism. The herbs contained within the compound activate the many processes required to metabolize fat and stimulate circulation while correcting the underlying imbalances of the Kapha constitution, which may eventually lead to sluggishness and congestion.

DOSAGE

Take 30-60 drops (½-1 teaspoon) 3 times daily in a small amount of warm water between meals.

CONTRAINDICATIONS/CAUTIONS

Do not use these herbs during pregnancy and lactation.

Single Herb Uses

Aconite
Aconitum napellus

A valuable remedy for facial and trigeminal neuralgia. Also eases the arthritic or gouty pain often associated with neuralgia. CAUTION: For professional use only.

Alfalfa Leaf
Medicago sativa

Alfalfa leaves are rich in protein, calcium and trace minerals, carotene, and vitamins E and K. They are a rich source of weak plant phytoestrogens, useful in balancing the hormones when treating hyper- and hypo-estrogenism.

Angelica Root
Angelica archangelica

Angelica is a useful expectorant for coughs, bronchitis, and pleurisy, especially when accompanied by colds, fever, or flu. It also eases intestinal colic and flatulence, stimulates appetite, and may be used in anorexia nervosa. It is helpful in easing rheumatic inflammations and acts as a urinary antiseptic in cystitis.

Arnica Flowers
Arnica latifolia

Taken internally, arnica is potentially toxic and can cause blistering of the intestinal mucosa. Externally, it is useful in treating any kind of pain or inflammation of the skin, as long as the skin is not broken. Use on bruises and sprains and to relieve the pain and inflammation of phlebitis and rheumatism.

Ashwagandha
Withenia somnifera

This herb is considered the Ginseng of India in Ayurvedic medicine. It is adaptogenic and strengthens the body's power of resistance. It builds immunity and is useful as a general tonic to enhance virility and vitality.

Astragalus Root/Huang Qi
Astragalus membranaceus

Tones the spleen and is useful in spleen deficiency problems such as poor appetite, fatigue, and diarrhea. Also useful for prolapse syndromes such as prolapsed uterus, stomach, or anus, and also for uterine bleeding. Is an effective diuretic and promotes the discharge of pus.

Barberry Root Bark
Berberis vulgaris

An excellent remedy for correcting liver function and promoting bile flow. Use for gall bladder inflammation, gall stones, and jaundice (when due to a congested liver). Barberry can reduce an enlarged spleen and can strengthen and cleanse a debilitated system.

Bayberry Bark
Myrica cerifera

Bayberry's astringent qualities make it valuable in treating diarrhea and dysentery. Useful for mucous colitis, as a gargle for sore throats, and a douche for treating leukorrhea.

Black Cohosh Root
Cimicifuga racemosa

Black Cohosh is a powerful relaxant which is very useful in the treatment of rheumatic pains, osteo-arthritis, muscular and neurological pain, and rheumatoid neuralgia. It also exerts a strong influence on the female reproductive system, normalizing menstruation and relieving menstrual cramps.

Black Haw Root and Tree Bark
Viburnum prunifolium

Black Haw Root is a powerful antispasmodic and nervine, acting particularly well on the uterus. It is used for dysmenorrhea, false labor pains, and in threatened miscarriage. It can also relax peripheral blood vessels and is used to reduce high blood pressure.

Black Walnut Hulls
Juglans nigra

A powerful remedy for expelling worms and also an antifungal, useful in treating candida, pin worms, ringworm, and tapeworms. Also a mild laxative, and useful for treatment of skin problems such as eczema and herpes.

Bladderwrack Fronds
Fucus vesiculosis

Bladderwrack regulates thyroid function and is effective in treating under-active thyroid glands, goiter, and all associated symptoms. Also helps relieve rheumatism and rheumatoid arthritis.

Blessed Thistle Herb
Cnicus benedictus

Primarily effective in treating female problems such as painful menstruation and associated headache. Stimulates menstruation, and is an excellent promoter of abundant breast milk especially when combined with Red Raspberry Leaves. Also stimulates gastric secretions, helping digestion.

Bloodroot
Sanguinaria canadensis

Bloodroot is valuable in treating congestive lung conditions such as chronic bronchitis and emphysema, acting to stimulate deficient peripheral circulation. At the same time it relaxes bronchial muscles and is useful in treating asthma, croup, and laryngitis.

Blue Cohosh
Caulophyllum thalictroides

An antispasmodic, Blue Cohosh is an excellent, safe herb for toning the uterus, easing false labor pains and dysmenorrhea, and can be used for threatened miscarriage. Its antispasmodic properties are also useful in treating colic, asthma, or nervous coughs.

Blue Flag Root
Iris versicolor

Useful in treating a variety of skin diseases such as eczema and psoriasis, Blue Flag helps the skin by aiding the liver in its detoxifying work. Also valuable for constipation when it is caused by liver problems or biliousness.

Blue Vervain
Verbena hastata

Vervain is a tonic for the nervous system and is, at the same time, a sedative useful in easing tension, depression, hysteria, and seizure. It promotes moderate perspiration useful in fevers, reduces inflammation of the gallbladder, and is helpful in treating jaundice.

Boneset Herb
Eupatorium perfoliatum

Boneset is excellent in relieving the aches and pains from the flu. It is also helpful to the body in coping with any accompanying fever and clears mucous congestion from the upper respiratory tract.

Buchu Leaves
Barosma betulina

Acts as a diuretic and urinary antiseptic, helpful in any genitourinary system infection such as cystitis, urethritis, and prostatitis. Heals and soothes also.

Buckthorn Bark
Rhamnus cathartica

A stimulant and cathartic causing bowel movements, used mostly as a laxative but also as a bitter tonic to ease digestive problems.

Bugleweed Herb
Lycopus virginica

Used in treating overactive thyroid glands, especially when accompanied by tightness of breath, palpitations, and shaking. An effective nervine, Bugleweed helps calm both palpitations and coughs that are of nervous origin.

Burdock Root
Arctium lappa

Burdock is quite effective in treating dry and scaly skin disorders such as psoriasis, dandruff, and eczema, particularly when they are caused by a general systemic imbalance. It stimulates the digestive juices and bile secretion and therefore is useful in treating anorexia nervosa and digestion and appetite problems. Burdock also aids liver function and is used to heal cystitis.

Butterbur Root
Petasites frigida

Butterbur has spasmolytic and pain-relieving properties, with a beneficial effect on acute and chronic gastritis and gastroduodenitis, gastro-cardiac syndrome, and painful spasms in the biliary tract.

Calamus Root
Acorus calamus

A powerful herb with a tonic effect on the stomach, promoting secretory activity and stimulating appetite. Very effective in treating appetite loss in conditions such as anorexia, childhood umbilical colic, and all kinds of appetite disorders.

Calendula Flowers
Calendula officinalis

Calendula is one of the most valuable herbs in the treatment of external skin problems like slow healing wounds, skins ulcers, inflammation, or minor burns. Internally it reduces digestive inflammation and therefore is helpful in treating gastric and duodenal ulcers. Also useful for relieving indigestion and gallbladder problems, and can help normalize delayed or painful menstruation.

California Poppy
Eschscholzia california

Useful in treating sleeplessness and over excitability in children, acting as a sedative. California Poppy is a non-addictive alternative to the Opium Poppy and may be used as a general antispasmodic.

Cascara Sagrada Bark
Rhamnus purshiana

Used as a laxative in treating chronic constipation, where it promotes peristalsis and tones relaxed digestive system muscles.

Catnip Herb
Nepeta cataria

Commonly used in relieving colds and flu, Catnip promotes moderate perspiration and therefore is helpful in treating fevers and in particular acute bronchitis. Catnip is also antispasmodic and relieves stomach upset, dyspepsia, flatulence, and colic. It is an excellent remedy for diarrhea in children, and is a useful sedative.

Catuaba
Juniperus brasiliensis

Rainforest botanical. Useful as a male aphrodisiac and a tonic to the male organs. It is also a strong tonic and fortifier of the nervous system.

Celandine Tops and Roots
Chelidonium majus

Celandine promotes the flow of bile, stimulates the pancreas, and is effective in gallbladder problems, hepatitis, jaundice, gallstones, and inflammatory conditions of the biliary system.

Chamomile Flowers, German
Matricaria chamomilla

Chamomile is an excellent nervine that relaxes and tones the nervous system and is especially useful in treating digestive problems such as gas, colic, or ulcers produced by anxiety. It is safe for children of all ages in treating nervousness or teething pain, and can be added to the bath water. Chamomile is a sleep aid, a mild anti-microbial, and an anti-catarrhal helpful in removing excess mucous in the sinus area.

Chaparral Leaf
Larrea tridentata
Chaparral sedates inflammation of the respiratory and intestinal tracts and relieves the pain of neuritis, sciatica, and inflammations, and has antibacterial properties.

Chaste Tree Berry
Vitex agnus-castus
Normalizes and stimulates pituitary gland functions, particularly those of the female sex hormones; effective on dysmenorrhea, premenstrual stress, and especially menopausal changes.

Chickweed Herb
Stellaria media
Useful in treating cuts, wounds, itching, and irritation, particularly when the irritation is caused by eczema or psoriasis. Internally helpful with rheumatism.

Chuchuhuasi
Maytenus krukovit
Rainforest botanical. Used to relieve symptoms associated with rheumatoid arthritis. Also useful as a muscle relaxant, effective in breaking up and dispersing lactic acid.

Cinnamon Bark
Cinnamomum zeylanicum
This bark is a useful carminative agent aiding in the removal of gas in the digestive tract. It acts as a stomachic in aiding

the digestive processes. It is an effective styptic, and can be used as such with uterine hemorrhaging.

Cleavers Herb
Galium aparine

An excellent lymphatic system tonic with alterative and diuretic properties, Cleavers works safely on a variety of lymphatic problems such as swollen glands (especially in tonsillitis and adenoid ailments). Useful in treating ulcers and tumors, since it aids lymphatic drainage and therefore detoxifies the tissue. Cleavers also is effective on painful urinary conditions such as cystitis.

Codonopsis Root/Tang Shen Root
Codonopsis tangshen

Benefits the lungs and is helpful in treating chronic cough and shortness of breath. Also tones the spleen and helps deficient conditions such as tired limbs, diarrhea, vomiting, and lack of appetite.

Cola Nut
Cola nitida

Stimulates the central nervous system and is helpful in cases of nervous debility, depression, and nervous diarrhea. May be used with other herbs to treat anorexia.

Collinsonia Root
Collinsonia canadensis

Collinsonia stimulates, cleanses, and tones the mucous membranes of the digestive system and is helpful in gastro-enteritis with diarrhea and in hemorrhoids. It is also slightly astringent, relieving inflammations of the throat, flu, chronic pleurisy, and colds.

Comfrey Leaf
Symphytum officinalis

An excellent demulcent which stimulates cell proliferation, useful in speeding the healing of gastric and duodenal ulcers, hiatus hernia, and ulcerative colitis. Very high nutritive properties.

Comfrey Root
Symphytum officinalis

Same as Comfrey Leaf, but higher in mucilage which soothes and protects irritated or inflamed internal tissue.

Corn Silk
Zea mays

Corn Silk is a gentle diuretic, useful in treating urinary problems in children. It acts as a urinary demulcent when combined with other herbs to treat urinary ailments like cystitis, urethritis, and prostatitis.

Cramp Bark
Viburnum opulus

An excellent antispasmodic, Cramp Bark works to relax muscular cramps in general and works on the uterine and ovarian muscles in particular. By relaxing uterine muscles it relieves menstrual cramps and can help in threatened miscarriage. Its astringent properties are effective in treating excessive blood loss during menstruation and menopausal bleeding.

Damiana Herb
Turnera diffusa

Acts as a tonic on the central nervous system and the hormonal system. Used in treating depression and anxiety, particularly when influenced by sexual factors. Strengthens the male sexual system.

Dandelion Root
Taraxacum officinalis

Dandelion is an excellent, safe diuretic and liver tonic. Dandelion is a valuable diuretic because it is rich in potassium, a vital mineral often lost when the kidneys are stimulated by drugs. It is useful in treating water retention due to heart problems, inflammation and congestion of the liver and gall-bladder, and congestive jaundice.

Devil's Claw Root
Harpagophytum procumbens

Devil's Claw has antiinflammatory properties which may help some cases of arthritis with inflammation and pain. Also acts as a hepatic in treating liver and gallbladder problems.

Devil's Club Root Bark
Oplopanax horridum

This herb is used as a blood sugar stabilizing agent. It is used routinely in the treatment of diabetes as a natural alternative to insulin.

Dong Quai Root/Dang Gui
Angelica sinensis

Tones the blood and invigorates the circulatory system, acting on conditions such as palpitations, carbuncles or pain from congealed blood, abdominal pain, and traumatic injuries. Also helps with irregular menstruation, amenorrhea, and dysmenorrhea.

Dusty Miller
Cineraria maritima

Use in treating eye ailments such as conjunctivitis where it induces a low degree of hyperemia. Also helpful in the early stages of senile cataract, especially when the vision is generally weak.

Elderberry Flowers
Sambucus canadensis

Colds and flu respond well to Elder Flowers, which are also helpful in treating upper respiratory tract inflammations such as sinusitis and hay fever.

Elecampane Root
Inula helenium

Useful in treating irritating bronchial coughs such as those that occur in bronchitis or emphysema, especially in children. Elecampane aids expectoration and at the same time has a soothing action. It can also be used in treating asthma, bronchitic asthma, and tuberculosis.

Ephedra Twigs/Ma Huang
Ephedra sinica

Opens the pores and promotes perspiration, useful in treating chills, fever, headache, and tight, floating pulse. Also helpful in controlling wheezing and relaxes the lungs. Promotes urination and reduces edema.

Espinhiera Santa
Maytenus ilicifolia

Rainforest botanical. Regulates stomach hydrochloric acid production and is therefore useful for stomach ulcers, especially those produced by nervousness. Other effects on the digestive system include its ability to restore intestinal flora, inhibit pathogenic bacteria, produce laxative effects, and benefit colic.

Eyebright Herb
Euphrasia officinalis

Eyebright has an antiinflammatory action combined with astringent properties which make it a powerful treatment for congestive illnesses such as nasal catarrh and sinusitis. It is also used in treating eye conditions such as chronic or acute inflammations, stinging and weeping eyes, and over-sensitivity to light.

Fennel Seed
Foeniculum vulgare

Excellent in treating stomach and intestinal problems such as flatulence, colic, and lack of appetite. Calms bronchitis and coughs and stimulates milk flow in nursing mothers.

Fenugreek Seed
Trigonella foenum-graecum

Valuable in healing and reducing inflammations in wounds; eases bronchitis and sore throats; soothes digestive problems and stimulates milk production in nursing mothers.

Feverfew Herb
Chrysanthemum parthenium

A valuable herb in the treatment of migraine headaches as well as relieving some of the accompanying symptoms such as nausea, depression, and arthritic pain due to inflammation. Feverfew may also help ease dizziness, tinnitus, arthritis in its active inflammatory stage, and painful or sluggish menstruation. CAUTION: Do not use during pregnancy because of the stimulating action on the womb.

Figwort
Scrophularia nodosa

Used primarily to treat skin problems such as psoriasis and eczema, acting as a general cleanser of the total body system. Acts as a mild laxative and diuretic. Avoid Figwort in cases of abnormally rapid heartbeat (tachycardia).

Fo-Ti Root/He Shou Wu
Polygonum multiflorum

Fo-Ti is astringent and helps treat conditions such as nocturnal emission, spermatorrhea, or leukorrhea. It also tones the liver and kidneys as well as the blood.

Fringe Tree
Chionanthus virginicus

Valuable in treating all liver problems. Gallbladder inflammation, gall-stones, and jaundice all respond well to Fringe Tree's action of stimulating the flow of bile from the liver.

Garlic
Allium sativum

Garlic is one of the most effective anti-microbial herbs, with both antibacterial and anti-viral properties. It acts on respiratory infections such as chronic bronchitis, respiratory catarrh, recurrent colds and flu, and is a powerful preventative for these conditions and for digestive infections as well. Garlic also lowers blood pressure, blood cholesterol levels, and acts as a tonic on the cardiovascular system.

Gelsemium Root
Gelsemium sempervirens

Gelsemium is a cardiac sedative for extra systoles and functional heart disease. CAUTION: For professional use only.

Gentian Root
Gentiana lutea

Excellent in treating sluggish digestion and lack of appetite, as indicated by conditions like dyspepsia and flatulence. Gentian stimulates the appetite and digestion and promotes the production of saliva, gastric juices, and bile.

Geranium Root
Geranium maculatum

Used primarily as an astringent in diarrhea, dysentery, and hemorrhoids. May be used with other herbs to treat bleeding duodenal or gastric ulcers. Also acts to reduce blood loss during menstruation or uterine hemorrhage.

Ginger Root
Zingiber officinalis

Ginger acts as a peripheral circulation stimulant and is helpful in treating bad circulation, chilblains, and cramps. It is also used as a remedy for digestive problems, sore throats, and as a promoter of perspiration in treating fever.

Ginkgo Leaf
Ginkgo biloba

Ginkgo has a powerful effect on brain function and cerebral circulation and acts on wide range of vascular conditions. Some of these include vertigo, tinnitus, neurological disorders, Alzheimer's disease, memory and concentration problems, diminished intellectual capacity due to insufficient circulation, and complications of stroke and skull injuries.

Ginseng Root, Siberian
Eleutherococcus senticosus

Increases resistance to damaging external environmental

factors and to illnesses, and increases vitality. Reduces incidence of flu, acute respiratory disease, hypertension, ischemic heart disease, etc. Excellent as a general tonic.

Ginseng Root, Wild American and Woods-Grown American
Panax quinquifolium

Ginseng increases vitality and improves the body's resistance to a wide variety of illnesses and damaging external influences. Especially helpful to weak or elderly people.

Goat's Rue
Galega officinalis

Goat's Rue herb is primarily used as a lactagogue, increasing milk production in the nursing mother. It has also been used as a cathartic, diuretic, diaphoretic, and to treat sprains and dislocation.

Goldenrod Flowering Tops
Solidago canadensis/odora

A valuable herb in treating upper respiratory ailments such as cough, flu, and bronchitis due to its stimulating and slightly astringent action on the mucous membranes. Goldenrod is also a urinary antiinflammatory helpful in treating conditions like cystitis and urethritis.

Goldenseal Root
Hydrastis canadensis

Effective in all digestive problems from peptic ulcers to colitis due to its tonic effects on the body's mucous membranes. Goldenseal is a powerful anti-microbial improving all catarrhal conditions, especially those of the sinuses.

Gotu Kola Leaf and Root
Centella asiatica

Gotu Kola is a stimulant to the central nervous system and is used to improve memory and treat fatigue.

Gravel Root
Eupatorium purpureum

Used in treating kidney stones (gravel), and also helpful in urinary infections such as cystitis and urethritis.

Grindelia Floral Buds
Grindelia robusta

Acting as a relaxant on smooth muscles and heart muscles, Grindelia is useful in treating asthmatic and bronchial conditions, especially when accompanied by rapid heart beat and nervousness. Blood pressure may go down with Grindelia.

Helonias Root
Chamaelirium luteum

An excellent tonic and strengthener of the reproductive systems for both sexes, although used primarily for women. Normalizes functions, tones, and balances. Useful in delayed or absent menstruation, in ovarian pain, to prevent miscarriage, and to ease vomiting associated with pregnancy.

Hops Strobile
Humulus lupulus

Hops relaxes the central nervous system and is an excellent remedy for insomnia, tension, and anxiety. CAUTION: Should be avoided in cases with marked depression, which may be accentuated by this herb.

Horehound Herb
Marrubium vulgare

Valuable as an expectorant, promoting mucous production which can ease upper respiratory ailments such as bronchitis, whooping cough, and colds.

Horse Chestnut
Aesculus hippocastanum

The actions of horse chestnut are astringent and antiinflammatory, influencing largely the vessels of the circulatory system. It is a useful remedy for vascular fullness associated with hemorrhoids, varicose veins, rectal engorgement, phlebitis, and leg ulcers.

Horseradish Root
Amoracia rusticana

This herb contains volatile oils effecting the sinus cavity and mucous membranes. It acts as a stimulant increasing secretions of these membranes and therefore is useful in sinus congestion. It is also useful in the treatment of laryngitis.

Horsetail Herb
Equisetum arvense

Horsetail acts on the genito-urinary system as an astringent which can reduce hemorrhaging and heal wounds. It is also a mild diuretic with toning and astringent properties, making it an effective treatment for incontinence and bed-wetting in children.

Hydrangea Root
Hydrangea spp.

Excellent in treating inflamed or enlarged prostate glands. Also acts as a sedative in urinary irritations and painful kidney stones associated with urinary infections.

Hyssop Flowering Herb
Hyssopus officinalis

Hyssop is useful in coughs, bronchitis, and chronic catarrh due to its antispasmodic action. It also acts as nervine helpful in treating anxiety, hysteria, and petit mal.

Jamaican Dogwood
Piscidia erythrina

A powerful sedative used primarily for insomnia due to nervous tension or pain. Helpful in treating the pain of neuralgia and migraine. Also relieves ovarian and uterine pain.

Jambul Seed
Syzygium jambolanum

Jambul Seed is useful in treating diabetes, and also is used as a carminative, stomachic, and diuretic.

Juniper Berry
Juniperus communis

An excellent diuretic with anti-microbial properties, useful in conditions such as cystitis. Its bitter action helps digestion and eases flatulent colic. CAUTION: Avoid in any kidney disease and during pregnancy.

Kava Kava Root
Piper methysticum

Kava Kava Root is a central nervous system depressant and a relaxant of the skeletal muscle which has no narcotic properties. It also anesthetizes the gastric and bladder mucosa and is useful in treating conditions such as irritable bladder syndrome.

Kelp Fronds
Nereocystis luetkeana

A very rich source of micronutrition, minerals, and trace minerals. Especially high in iodine and potassium, useful for underactive thyroid function and for alkalizing blood chemistry.

Lavender Flowering Herb
Lavandula officinalis

Effective in treating headaches, especially those due to stress. Lavender is a valuable antidepressant which also strengthens the nervous system and helps cases of nervous debility and exhaustion.

Lemon Balm
Melissa officinalis

Lemon Balm is a nervine which eases digestive tract spasms and is useful in flatulent dyspepsia. It also has mild antidepressive properties and helps in tension, depression, migraine, anxiety-induced palpitations, and insomnia.

Licorice Root
Glycyrrhiza glabra

Acts on the endocrine system and the liver as an antihepatotoxic effective in treating hepatitis and cirrhosis. Licorice is also an expectorant and antiinflammatory, useful in cough and bronchitis.

Life Root
Senecio aureus

A tonic acting especially well on the female reproductive

organs, Life Root is a safe, strengthening herb that is especially useful in treating menopausal disturbances. It also helps with delayed or suppressed menstruation and leukorrhea.

Ligustrum Berry/Nu Zhen Zi
Ligustrum lucidum

Nourishes and tones the liver and kidney, acting on conditions such as dizziness, spots in front of the eyes, lower back pain, and tinnitus.

Lily of the Valley
Convallaria majalis

Lily of the Valley is a cardiac tonic which increases coronary circulation and myocardial action, useful in treating conditions such as congestive heart failure, cardiac asthma, and mitral insufficiency. Appropriate for all cardiac disturbances, especially conditions of incipient decompensation. CAUTION: For professional use only.

Linden Flowers
Tilia spp.

Linden is valuable in the treatment of nervous tension and its relaxing properties are also helpful in some forms of migraine. Linden can prevent the development of arteriosclerosis and hypertension and is often used to treat high blood pressure when associated with arteriosclerosis and nervous tension.

Lobelia Herb and Seed
Lobelia inflata

Lobelia is a valuable systemic relaxant, with a depressant action on the central and autonomic nervous systems. It is primarily used in bronchitic asthma and bronchitis, where it acts as a respiratory relaxant while at the same time stimulates catarrhal secretion and expectoration. CAUTION: For professional use only.

Lomatium Root
Lomatium dissectum

An effective anti-viral and antibacterial, especially useful in the treatment of respiratory and urinary infections. Lomatium stimulates the immune system and decreases inflammation.

Lungwort Lichen
Sticta pulmonaria

High in mucilage, and is indicated in respiratory conditions such as chronic bronchial cough and asthma. Also a bitter, promoting gastric juice secretions and useful for patients whose health is poor due to protracted cough.

Madagascar Periwinkle
Vinca rosea

A rich source of vincrisdine and vindblastine two alkaloids now being used as chemotherapeutic agents in the treatment of Hodgkin's disease.

Marshmallow Root
Althaea officinalis

Marshmallow soothes inflamed tissue in the digestive system, helping conditions such as inflammations of the mouth, gastritis, peptic ulceration, and colitis.

Meadowsweet Herb
Filipendula ulmaria

An excellent remedy for digestive complaints such as nausea, heartburn, hyperacidity, gastritis, and peptic ulcers. Also has gentle astringency useful for childhood diarrhea. Contains aspirin-like chemicals which relieve fever and rheumatic pain.

Melilot Flowering Herb
Melilotus officinalis

Melilot soothes the stomach and is useful for treating chronic flatulence, particularly following intestinal infections.

Milk Thistle Seed
Silybum marianum

Excellent as a liver tonic and in treating numerous liver and gallbladder conditions such as hepatitis and cirrhosis. May also reverse toxic liver damage and protect against hepatotoxic agents.

Mistletoe Herb
Viscum flavenscens

Has gentle hypotensive properties affecting parasympathetic stimulation and vasodilation, useful in treating symptoms associated with hypertension such as headaches, dizziness, loss of energy, and irritability, and in treating mild cases of hypertension. CAUTION: For professional use only.

Motherwort Flowering Herb
Leonurus cardiaca

Motherwort is a nervine particularly effective in treating menstrual and uterine conditions, especially those influenced by anxiety or tension such as delayed or suppressed menstruation, menopausal changes, and false labor pains. It is also effective in treating heart palpitations, especially caused by tension, and is an excellent heart tonic.

Mugwort Herb
Artemisia vulgaris

Mugwort is a digestive aid, acting through the bitter stimulation of digestive juices. Mildly relaxing, it is useful in treating depression and nervous tension.

Muira Puama Root
Ptychopetalum olacoides

Rainforest botanical. Muira Puama is known as "Potency Wood," a plant which activates sexual virility. It is also known for its aphrodisiac properties and is used for genital weakness.

Mullein Leaf and Flowers
Verbascum thapsus

Mullein is excellent in treating upper respiratory conditions such as bronchitis due to its tonic action on mucous membranes of the respiratory system. It also reduces inflammation of the trachea and at the same time soothes inflamed tissues.

Myrrh Gum
Commiphora molmol

Myrrh's anti-microbial action is especially effective in mouth infections such as gingivitis, in sinusitis, laryngitis, and respiratory complaints. Often used in treating the common cold. Also helpful in systemic conditions like boils, glandular fever, and brucellosis.

Nettle Leaf
Urtica dioica

Nettles affect a wide range of ailments and act as a tonic and general detoxifying remedy for the whole body. They excel in treating some cases of rheumatism and arthritis, and also are beneficial in all varieties of eczema, particularly childhood eczema, and in cases caused by nervous tension.

Night-Blooming Cereus
Cactus grandiflorus

Night Blooming Cereus is a stimulating cardiac tonic which raises the blood pressure and regulates the pulse. Effective in conditions such cardiac weakness, low blood pressure, anemia, and angina.

Oats, Wild, Milky Seed
Avena sativa

An excellent remedy for strengthening the entire nervous system, oats are used in treating nervous debility, exhaustion when associated with depression, and stress.

Oregon Grape Root
Berberis aquifolium

Acts as a tonic on the liver and gallbladder and can remedy chronic and scaly skin problems such as psoriasis and eczema which are caused by systemic imbalances. Also helpful for stomach and gallbladder conditions, especially when associated with vomiting and nausea.

Osha Root
Ligusticum porterii

An excellent herb for treating viral infections, producing thorough perspiration and elimination of toxins. Useful for bronchial inflammations and sore throats, acting to soothe sore tissues while also promoting expectoration.

Parsley Leaf and Root
Petroselinum crispum

Parsley is a diuretic, can ease flatulence and the accompanying colic pains, and can stimulate the menstrual process. CAUTION: Do not use in medicinal dosage during pregnancy.

Passionflower
Passiflora incarnata

As a sedative, passionflower is the preferred herb for treating insomnia and leaves no hangover. As an antispasmodic, it is helpful in Parkinson's disease, asthma (with much spasmodic activity), seizures, and hysteria. It relieves nerve pain in conditions like neuralgia and shingles.

Pau D'Arco Inner Bark
Tabebuia impetiginosa

A South American tree bark which has strong anti-fungal and anti-yeast properties, used as a blood alterative, prophylactically, and in chronic health imbalances.

Pennyroyal
Mentha pulegium

Useful primarily as a uterine stimulant, to strengthen uterine contractions during labor, and to start the menstrual process. Also eases flatulence and abdominal colic caused by wind. CAUTION: Avoid during pregnancy.

Peppermint Leaf
Mentha piperita

Peppermint relaxes the muscles of the digestive system, relieving conditions like flatulence, intestinal colic, and flatulent dyspepsia. It also acts as a mild anesthetic to the stomach wall and is useful in treating nausea and vomiting. It can relieve nasal catarrh and is used in colds, fevers, and flu. Peppermint is also a nervine helpful in easing painful periods and lessening anxiety.

Periwinkle Herb
Vinca minor

Excellent as an astringent, used primarily in treating excessive menstrual flow and similar problems in the urinary system such as hematuria. Its astringency reduces the loss of fluid or blood in digestive conditions such as colitis or diarrhea. It also is effective in treating nose bleeds, bleeding gums, mouth ulcers, or sore throats.

Pipsissewa Herb
Chimaphila umbellata

A urinary antiseptic and a diuretic with a beneficial effect on the liver, kidney, and bladder. Pipsissewa also has astringent properties making it useful in treating conditions such as diarrhea.

Plantain Leaf and Corm
Plantago lanceolata

Plantain is an astringent, acting to reduce fluids in a variety of conditions including diarrhea, dysentery, hemorrhoids, excessive menstrual flow, and hematuria. It is also a gentle expectorant which soothes inflamed membranes, helping in coughs, mild bronchitis, and inflammation of the intestinal tract.

Pleurisy Root
Asclepias tuberosa

Valuable in treating all kinds of respiratory infections such as pneumonia, pleurisy, flu, and bronchitis. Pleurisy Root reduces inflammation, promotes moderate perspiration, and aids expectoration.

Poke Root
Phytolacca americana

Poke Root is a remedy for upper respiratory infections, useful in treating cough, tonsillitis, laryngitis, swollen glands, and mumps. It cleans the lymphatic glands throughout the body and is especially helpful in mastitis. It is also used for rheumatism. CAUTION: In large doses, Poke Root is a powerful emetic and purgative (causes vomiting). For professional use only.

Prickly Ash Bark
Xanthoxylum clava-herculis

Stimulates the circulation, lymphatic system, and mucous membranes; effective in chilblains, leg cramp, varicose veins and ulcers, rheumatism, and skin diseases.

Propolis
Bee-Harvested Tree Resin

A strong anti-microbial, antibacterial, and anti-viral agent used topically and in the treatment of wounds, injuries, and infections. Very useful as a first-aid remedy.

Pygeum Bark
Pygeum africanum

Effective in the treatment of benign prostate hyperplasia or prostatic inflammation.

Quebra Pedra
Phyllanthus niruri

Rainforest botanical. Quebra Pedra has been historically used to clear obstruction throughout the system by promoting the elimination of mucous and calculi (kidney stones). It is believed to strengthen and fortify liver and gall bladder function by stimulating the production of bile.

Red Clover Blossoms
Trifolium pratense

A safe and effective treatment for childhood eczema. Also useful for chronic skin problems in children and adults such as psoriasis. An expectorant and antispasmodic, Red Clover works especially well on whooping cough and also on coughs and bronchitis.

Red Raspberry Leaves
Rubus idaeus

Valuable as a strengthener and toner of the womb during pregnancy, and helpful in restraining hemorrhage during labor and assisting contractions. Its astringent action is also helpful in reducing fluids for a variety of other conditions including diarrhea, leukorrhea, and mouth problems such as bleeding gums and inflammations.

Red Root
Ceanothus americanus

Red Root stimulates lymph and intertissue fluid circulation and is effective on tonsil inflammations, sore throats, enlarged lymph nodes, and for shrinking non-fibrous cysts. It also has astringent properties useful in stopping menstrual hemorrhage, nose bleeds, bleeding piles, hemorrhoids, and capillary ruptures from vomiting or coughing.

Rose Hips
Rosa rugosa

An astringent affecting primarily the kidneys, bladder, and

colon, controlling diarrhea and reducing urine excretion and intestinal leakage. Helps to stabilize the kidneys.

Rosemary Leaf
Rosmarinus officinalis

Rosemary calms and tones the digestive system helping ease conditions like flatulent dyspepsia. It also helps with nervous tension which may manifest in headache or depression.

Rue
Ruta graveolens

Rue acts primarily on the uterus, bringing on suppressed menstruation; it is a powerful abortifacient. It is also used to relax the muscles of the digestive system, easing griping and bowel tension. The antispasmodic action also helps to stop spasmodic coughs. CAUTION: Avoid during pregnancy.

Sage Leaf
Salvia officinalis

Sage is excellent in reducing inflammations of the mouth, throat, and tonsils and is used in treating ailments such as gingivitis, mouth ulcers, laryngitis, and tonsillitis. It is also helpful in dyspepsia. CAUTION: Avoid during pregnancy.

Sarsaparilla Root
Smilax officinalis v. omata

Gradually restores the proper functioning of the body, correcting a wide range of systemic problems. These include scaling skin conditions such as psoriasis, and rheumatic conditions. Especially useful for rheumatoid arthritis.

Saw Palmetto Berry
Serenoa repens

Acts as a tonic and strengthener of the male reproductive system, and is helpful in treating enlarged prostate glands. Also useful in genito-urinary tract infections.

Schizandra Berry/Wu Wei Zi
Schizandra chinensis

Strengthens and quickens reflexes, stimulates respiration, and is useful in promoting labor. Also reduces perspiration, stops coughing and diarrhea.

Scotch Broom
Cytisus scoparius

Diuretic, cathartic, and emetic in large doses, Scotch Broom has also been found to be effective in the treatment of mild hypertension and tumors.

Sheep Sorrel
Rumex acetosella

This herb has been popularized as a key ingredient in Renee Caisse's Essiac formula. Eclectic references suggest it has a marked influence on "tissue of lower organization" and thus is useful for degenerative tissues throughout the body.

Shepherd's Purse
Capsella bursa-pastoris

Acts as an astringent in conditions such as diarrhea, wounds, nose bleeds, and excessive menstrual flow, while at the same time is useful in stimulating suppressed menstruation. Also useful as a gentle diuretic.

Skullcap Herb
Scutellaria laterifolia

An excellent nervine for a wide range of ailments. Skullcap relaxes while also revivifying the central nervous system. Valuable in treating seizure, hysteria, and epilepsy. A safe treatment for easing premenstrual tension.

Chinese Skullcap
Scutellaria baicalensis

Chinese Skullcap is anti-microbial, antipyretic, and antiinflammatory. It is used for treating high fevers and accompanying irritability, thirst, cough, and expectoration of sputum. Also acts on the digestive system, easing diarrhea or dysentery-like disorders, and helps with painful urinary dysfunction.

Skunk Cabbage Root
Symplocarpus foetidus

An effective antispasmodic for lung ailments, easing and relaxing cough or lung tension in conditions such as asthma, bronchitis, and whooping cough. Also promotes moderate perspiration useful in treating fevers.

Slippery Elm Inner Bark
Ulmus rubra

Slippery Elm is useful in treating digestive conditions with inflamed mucous membrane linings such as gastritis, gastric or duodenal ulcer, enteritis, and colitis, where it has a soothing, demulcent action.

Spearmint
Mentha spicata

This herb is used in a similar way as peppermint, only

somewhat milder. It is an effective carminative aid to dispel gas in the digestive tract, and can be used as a mild diaphoretic.

Spilanthes Flowering Tops and Root
Spilanthes acmella

Promotes secretion of saliva and is useful in improving the appetite and digestive functions, overcoming nausea and vomiting, and eases flatulence.

Squaw Vine
Mitchella repens

An excellent herb to take during pregnancy to prepare the uterus and the whole body for a safe childbirth. Also used to relieve painful periods. Its astringency is effective in treating colitis, especially when accompanied by excess mucous.

St. Johnswort
Hypericum perforatum

A sedative and pain reducer useful in treating neuralgia, anxiety, depression, and in particular, irritability and tension due to menopausal changes. Also helpful in easing the pain of fibrositis, sciatica, and rheumatic pain.

Stillingia Root
Stillingia sylvatica

An excellent alterative acting primarily on the lymphatic and secretory systems, useful in treating any kind of laryngeal irritation, bronchitis, and syphilis.

Suma
Pfaffia paniculata

Rainforest botanical. Taken as a whole herb, Suma strengthens the immune system with active adaptogenic properties while discouraging the formation of tumors. It contains the trace element germanium and is a cellular oxygenator.

Tansy
Tanacetum vulgare

Acting primarily on the digestive system, tansy is effective in eliminating roundworm and thread worm, but is dangerous to use over a long period of time. Eases dyspepsia and is an enema treatment for children. Also may be used to stimulate menstruation. CAUTION: Avoid during pregnancy. For professional use only.

Thuja Leaf
Thuja occidentalis

Acts as an expectorant, useful in treating bronchial catarrh. When the catarrh is accompanied by heart weakness, Thuja Leaf is helpful since it also is a systemic stimulant, but it should be avoided if the catarrh is due to overstimulation. Also stimulates menstruation. CAUTION: Avoid during pregnancy.

Thyme Leaf
Thymus vulgaris

Stimulates and soothes the digestive system, helpful in easing dyspepsia and sluggish digestion. Its anti-microbial action is effective in sore throats, laryngitis, respiratory and digestive infections. An excellent cough remedy for bronchitis, whooping cough, and asthma.

Turmeric Root
Curcuma longa

Turmeric Root is a powerful gallbladder stimulant, promoting the flow of bile. Also stimulates gastric juices. A powerful antioxidant, antiinflammatory, and anti-hepatotoxic herb, useful in the treatment of inflammatory conditions such as diabetes, hepatitis, liver disorders, and skin conditions.

Una de Gato, Cat's Claw
Uncaria tomentosa

Rainforest botanical. A highly effective immune system stimulant that fights viral infection and diminishes chemical sensitivity. Una de Gato has been used to treat arthritis, bursitis, intestinal disorders, allergies, and to ease the side effects of chemotherapy.

Usnea Lichen
Usnea spp.

Old man's beard, as it is sometimes called, contains usneic acid, which is a strong respiratory and urinary antibiotic. This herb is useful in the treatment of bronchitis, pleurisy, and other respiratory infections, as well as being an effective treatment of urinary tract, kidney, and bladder infections.

Uva Ursi Leaf
Arctostaphylos uva ursi

Soothes, tones, and strengthens the membranes of the urinary system and is helpful in gravel or ulceration of the kidney or bladder, pyelitis, and cystitis.

Valerian Root
Valeriana officinalis

An excellent nervine for treating anxiety and tension, and a gentle, safe sleep aid. Valerian's antispasmodic action makes it a strong muscle relaxant used in muscle cramping, uterine cramps, and intestinal colic.

Venus' Flytrap
Dionaea muscipula

Stimulates and modulates the immune system, and reduces the growth rate of tumor tissue while increasing the number and activity of T-helper cells and other factors of the immune system. Helpful in treating conditions such as cancer, HIV, AIDS, or other degenerative or infectious diseases.

White Oak Bark
Quercus alba

A powerful astringent used primarily in treating diarrhea; also useful in dysentery and hemorrhoids, although it may be too strong for some conditions.

White Pine Bark
Pinus strobus

Used as an expectorant in the treatment of colds and upper respiratory conditions. White Pine Bark can also be used locally to simulate the healing of wounds.

Wild Cherry Bark
Prunus serotina

Wild Cherry is a strong sedative for the cough reflex and is part of the treatment for bronchitis, whooping cough, and all kinds of irritating cough. May also be combined with other herbs to treat asthma.

Wild Indigo Root
Baptisia tinctoria

Wild Indigo's anti-microbial action makes it useful in treating focused infections, particularly those of the ear, nose, and throat. Also used systemically to treat enlarged and inflamed lymph glands.

Wild Yam Root
Dioscorea villosa

A valuable antispasmodic used to relieve intestinal colic, diverticulitis, dysmenorrhea, and ovarian and uterine pains. Excellent as an antiinflammatory in treating rheumatoid arthritis.

Willow Bark
Salix spp.

A natural form of aspirin and used on similar conditions such as aches and pains, rheumatism, gout, and fever.

Witch Hazel Bark, Twigs, and Leaf
Hamamelis virginiana

Witch Hazel is used as an astringent to ease bleeding, hemorrhoids, bruises, inflamed swellings, dysentery, and varicose veins. It controls diarrhea.

Wood Betony
Stachys betonica

Wood Betony targets the nervous system and acts as a tonic and general relaxer. It is useful for anxiety and nervous tension associated with occasional headache and hypertension.

Wormseed
Chenopodium ambrosiodes

Wormseed is an aromatic herb with volatile oils effective in the treatment of worms, amoebas, and parasites. It is also a strong bitter agent influencing the secretions of the gastrointestinal tract.

Wormwood Herb
Artemisia absinthum

Wormwood's bitter action stimulates the digestive system, helping indigestion, especially when caused by gastric juice problems. A strong herb for treating worm infestations, particularly roundworm and pinworm.

Yarrow Flowers
Achillea millefolium

Promotes moderate perspiration helpful in relieving fevers. Lowers blood pressure, stimulates digestion, and tones blood vessels. Useful in treating urinary infections such as cystitis.

Yellow Dock Root
Rumex crispus

A valuable herb for treating chronic skin conditions such as psoriasis. Promotes the flow of bile and is used for jaundice when caused by congestion, is a blood cleanser, and a remedy for constipation.

Yerba Mate
Ilex paraguayiensis

Rainforest botanical. Yerba Mate is a stimulating general tonic to the body and mind. It is also used for its laxative and diuretic qualities.

Yerba Santa Leaf
Eriodictyon californicum

Yerba Santa is an expectorant and bronchial dilator, useful primarily in treating upper respiratory ailments such as asthma, pneumonia, and coughs. Also effective for mild bladder and urethra infections.

Yohimbe Bark
Corynanthe yohimbe

A rich source of strong alkaloids which block the uptake of neuro-transmitters at alpha-2 receptor sites, effective in dieting and weight management, Parkinson's disease, impotence, and lack of libido.

Yucca Root
Yucca spp.

Yucca is an antiinflammatory, useful in treating joint inflammation and arthritic pain. Can have a laxative effect.

Herbal Oils

Fresh Arnica Flower Oil

INGREDIENTS

Fresh arnica flowers, organic extra virgin olive oil

USES

Sore muscles, trauma.

Fresh Calendula Flower Oil

INGREDIENTS

Fresh calendula flowers, organic extra virgin olive oil

USES

Burns (sunburns or traumatic burns).

Comfrey Compounded Oil

INGREDIENTS

Fresh comfrey root, fresh marshmallow root, fresh mullein, fresh skullcap, fresh black walnut leaf, white oak bark, fresh gravel root, fresh lobelia herb and seed, fresh St. Johnswort flower bud oil, organic extra virgin olive oil

USES

Bruises, sprains, skin irritation (unbroken skin), soothing to inflamed tissue.

Fresh Garlic Oil

INGREDIENTS

Fresh organic garlic, organic extra virgin olive oil

USES

Ear pain, use as an ear drop.

Ginger Root Oil

INGREDIENTS

Fresh ginger, organic extra virgin olive oil

USES

Stimulates circulation, warming agent, arthritis pain.

Juniper Oil

INGREDIENTS

Fresh juniper berry, organic extra virgin olive oil

USES

Gouty arthritis, bone/joint soreness, penetrates skin easily.

Fresh Mullein Flower Oil

INGREDIENTS

Fresh mullein flowers, organic extra virgin olive oil

USES

Earache, pain from swelling of hemorrhoids.

Mullein/Hypericum Flower Oil

INGREDIENTS

Wildcrafted mullein flowers, St. Johnswort flower buds, fresh organic garlic, organic extra virgin olive oil

USES

Ear infection and pain.

Fresh Poke Root Oil

INGREDIENTS

Fresh poke root oil, organic extra virgin olive oil

USES

Breast mastitis (clogged milk ducts), use topically on breast, do not breast feed from this breast for 3-4 days following use.

Fresh St. Johnswort Flower Oil

INGREDIENTS

Fresh St. Johnswort flower buds, organic extra virgin olive oil

USES

Nerve injury or trauma, back injury.

Fresh Thuja Leaf Oil

INGREDIENTS

Fresh thuja leaf, organic extra virgin olive oil

USES

Warts, anti-microbial.

Compounded Herbal Salves

Comfrey Compounded

INGREDIENTS

Fresh comfrey root, fresh marshmallow root, fresh mullein, fresh skullcap, fresh black walnut leaf, white oak bark, fresh gravel root, fresh lobelia herb and seed, fresh St. Johnswort flower bud oil, organic extra virgin olive oil, pure beeswax

USES

Bruises, sprains, skin irritation (unbroken skin only), soothing to inflamed tissue.

Mullein/Lobelia Compounded

INGREDIENTS

Mullein leaf and flower, lobelia herb and seed, fresh poke root, organic extra virgin olive oil, pure beeswax

USES

Swollen glands, lymphatic engorgement.

Plantain/Goldenseal Compounded

INGREDIENTS

Fresh plantain leaf, fresh goldenseal root, fresh burdock root, fresh chaparral leaf, fresh black walnut leaf, fresh thuja leaf, turmeric root, bloodroot, eucalyptus essential oil, organic extra virgin olive oil, pure beeswax

USES

Antibiotic, use on infections, skin cancer.

The Herbal Repertory
Botanical Treatment Protocols

This clinical repertory is divided into the major body systems. Major imbalances are listed within each system with proper botanical treatments. This repertory provides an opportunity for the reader to become acquainted with a more clinical approach to medical herbalism. This section in no way supports an allopathic model of herbal usage. It is not intended to provide the reader with diagnostic or prescriptive advice for the treatment of specific illnesses. This information is solely for educational purposes. The remedies given are the collected information of materia medicas, U.S. Dispensatories, and clinical repertories as well as clinical experience. The reader should consult a fully licensed naturopathic physician for any medical condition present. This herbal repertory is not intended as a substitute for medical care.

Blood and Lymphatic System
Herbal Agents Influencing the Blood and Lymph

Anemia

Compounded Nutritional Elixir, Yellow Dock Root, Chlorella, Alfalfa Solid Extract

Blood Clots

Melilot Herb, Compounded Red Clover, Prickly Ash Bark, Compounded Echinacea/Red Root, Compounded Scudder's Alterative, Hawthorn

Blood Dyscrasia

Fresh Baptisia Root, Compounded Echinacea/Red Root, Fresh Thuja Leaf, Compounded Scudder's Alterative

Blood Poisoning

Compounded Echinacea, Lobelia Herb and Seed

Cancer

Compounded Hoxsey/Red Clover, Compounded Echinacea/
Red Root, Fresh Thuja Leaf, Astragalus Root, Fresh Yellow
Dock Root, Compounded Sheep Sorrel/Burdock

To the above add the following specifics:

Brain Cancer

Mistletoe Extract, Chaparral Extract, Venus' Flytrap
Extract

Breast Cancer

Fresh Goldenseal Root, Fresh Poke Root, Compounded
Echinacea, Fresh Blue Flag Root, Venus' Flytrap Extract

Colon/Liver/Pancreas Cancer

Chaparral Leaf, Turmeric Root Extract, Bromelain,
Venus' Flytrap Extract

Kidney Cancer

Mistletoe Extract, Turmeric Root Extract, Bromelain,
Venus' Flytrap Extract

Lung Cancer

Mistletoe Extract, Turmeric Root Extract, Fresh Poke
Root, Bromelain, Venus' Flytrap Extract

Prostate Cancer

Fresh Saw Palmetto Berry, Mistletoe Extract, Fresh
Poke Root, Turmeric Root Extract, Bromelain

Stomach Cancer

Turmeric Root Extract, Bromelain, Venus' Flytrap Extract

Uterine/Ovarian Cancer

Turmeric Root Extract, Bromelain, Fresh Poke Root Extract, Venus' Flytrap Extract

Caseated Lymph Nodes

Compounded Echinacea/Red Root, Fresh Poke Root Extract, Fresh Baptisia Root, Compounded Hoxsey/Red Clover, Goldenseal Root, Compounded Mullein/Lobelia Salve topically

Hodgkin's Disease

Madagascar Periwinkle, Compounded Hoxsey/Red Clover, Mistletoe Extract, Compounded Echinacea/Red Root, Turmeric Root Extract, Bromelain, Venus' Flytrap Extract

Leukemia

Compounded Echinacea/Red Root, Compounded Hoxsey/Red Clover, Fresh Baptisia Root, Fresh Thuja Leaf

Lymphatic Engorgement

Compounded Echinacea/Red Root, Fresh Thuja Leaf, Fresh Baptisia Root, Compounded Red Clover, Compounded Juniper Berry, Fresh Poke Root

Lymphatic Swelling

Compounded Echinacea/Red Root, Fresh Poke Root, Compounded Mullein/Lobelia Salve topically

Lymphedema

Fresh Cleavers Herb, Compounded Red Clover, Compounded Juniper Berry

Mastitis

Compounded Mullein/Lobelia Salve topically, Thuja Oil topically, Fresh Thuja Leaf, Compounded Echinacea/Red Root, Fresh Poke Root Oil topically, Fresh Poke Root

Cardiovascular System
Herbal Agents Influencing the Heart and Coronary Vascular System

Arrythmias

Hawthorn Berry Solid Extract, Compounded Hawthorn, Fresh Motherwort Extract, Lily of the Valley*, *Cactus grandiflorus* Extract

*Use only with physician's care.

Arteriosclerosis

Hawthorn Berry Solid Extract, Compounded Hawthorn, Bladderwrack Extract, Compounded Calcium Elixir

Angina Pectoris

Hawthorn Berry Solid Extract, Compounded Hawthorn, *Cactus grandiflorus* Extract

Cardiac Irritability

Compounded Bugleweed/Motherwort, Compounded Hawthorn, *Cactus grandiflorus* Extract

Congestive Heart Failure

Cactus grandiflorus Extract, Compounded Hawthorn

Hypertension

Compounded Linden/Crataegus, Hawthorn Berry Solid Extract, Compounded Hawthorn, Valerian Root, Wild Oats, Siberian Ginseng Root, Rauwolfia Root Extract

Hypotension

Siberian Ginseng Root, Fresh Wild Oats, Hawthorn Berry Solid Extract, *Cactus grandiflorus* Extract

Mitral Valve Insufficiency

Hawthorn Berry Solid Extract, *Cactus grandiflorus* Extract, Lily of the Valley*

*Use only with physician's care.

Nervous Heart

Compounded Hawthorn, Compounded Bugleweed/Motherwort, Compounded Calcium Elixir

Cardiac Palpitations

Compounded Bugleweed/Motherwort, Compounded Hawthorn

Pericarditis

Hawthorn Berry Solid Extract, Lily of the Valley*

*Use only with physician's care.

Tachycardia

Compounded Bugleweed/Motherwort, Compounded Hawthorn

Digestive System
Herbal Agents Influencing the Digestive Functions

Abdominal Pain – with pressure on pelvic viscera

Fringe Tree, Life Root, Fresh Helonias Root, Fresh Chaste Tree, Compounded Fraxinus/Ceanothus

Cirrhosis

Fringe Tree, Schizandra Berry, Milk Thistle Seed, *Eclipta alba*, *Phyllanthus amarus*

Dyspepsia

Compounded Elixir of Bitters, Glyconda Neutralizing Cordial

Gall Stones

Dandelion Root and Leaf, Compounded Dandelion/Fennel, Bladderwrack Extract, Fresh Gravel Root Extract, Compounded Fennel/Wild Yam

Gastritis

Fresh Gentian Root, Fennel Seed, Compounded Elixir of Bitters, Glyconda Neutralizing Cordial

Hepatitis

Milk Thistle Seed, Fringe Tree, Schizandra Berry, *Eclipta alba*, *Phyllanthus amarus*

Indigestion

Compounded Elixir of Bitters, Compounded Dandelion/Fennel, Glyconda Neutralizing Cordial

Jaundice

Fringe Tree

Pain – right-sided
Fresh Celandine Root and Tops, Compounded Elixir of Bitters, Dandelion Root, Glyconda Neutralizing Cordial

Pain – left-sided
Milk Thistle Seed, Red Root, Compounded Elixir of Bitters, Glyconda Neutralizing Cordial

Endocrine (Glandular) System
Herbal Agents Influencing the Glandular Functions

Pancreatitis
Turmeric Root Extract, Compounded Elixir of Bitters, Fringe Tree

Adrenal Insufficiency
Fresh Wild Oats, Licorice Root, Siberian Ginseng, Fo-Ti Extract, Compounded Elixir of Siberian Ginseng, Compounded Ginseng/Schizandra

Adrenal Exhaustion – with Cardiac Arrhythmias
Cactus grandiflorus Extract, Compounded Hawthorn

Lymphatics
See listing under Blood and Lymphatic System.

Mammary Glands

Cancer
Compounded Hoxsey/Red Clover, Compounded Echinacea/Red Root, Fresh Poke Root, Mistletoe Extract, Chaparral Extract, Turmeric Root Extract, Bromelain, Venus' Flytrap, Compounded Sheep Sorrel/Burdock

Fibroids

Fresh Thuja Leaf, Compounded Echinacea/Red Root, Fresh Poke Root, Fresh Goldenseal Root, Compounded Mullein/Lobelia Salve topically, Castor Oil topically, Fresh Poke Root Oil topically

Painful

Compounded Mullein/Lobelia salve topically, Castor oil topically

Pituitary Glands

Fresh Gotu Kola Leaf and Root, Compounded Gotu Kola, Chaste Tree Extract

Prostate Gland

See listing under Reproductive System.

Thyroid Gland

Goiter

Bladderwrack Extract, Fresh Thuja Leaf, Fresh Blue Flag Root, Mullein/Lobelia salve topically

Hypoactivity

Bladderwrack Extract

Grave's Disease

Compounded Calcium Elixir, Compounded Bugleweed/Motherwort, *Cactus grandiflorus* Extract, Compounded Hawthorn

Hyperactivity

Compounded Calcium Elixir, Compounded Bugleweed/Motherwort, Lemon Balm, Compounded Melissa

Gastrointestinal System
Herbal Agents Influencing the Colon and Small Intestine

Abdominal Bloating

Compounded Elixir of Bitters, Fennel Seed, Compounded Dandelion/Fennel, Glyconda Neutralizing Cordial

Colitis

Marshmallow Root, Licorice Root, Bowel Cleansing Powder, Robert's Formula, Slippery Elm

Colitis – Ulcerative

Bowel Cleansing Powder, Marshmallow Root, Licorice Root, Goldenseal Root, Compounded Echinacea, Robert's Formula, Slippery Elm

Constipation – with Deficient Glandular Secretions

Fresh Goldenseal Root, Prickly Ash Bark, Internal Cleansing Program (see below), Compounded Scudder's Alterative

Constipation – with Deficient Peristalsis

Bowel Cleansing Powder, Cascara Sagrada Bark, Compounded Scudder's Alterative

Constipation – with Flatulence

Butternut Bark, Fennel Seed, Compounded Bitter Elixir, Glyconda Neutralizing Cordial

Constipation – with Hardened Feces

Internal Cleansing Program (see below), Celandine Root and Tops (short-term use), Cascara Sagrada Bark, Compounded Scudder's Alterative

Diarrhea – with Mucous and Coldness

Ginger Root, Red Raspberry Leaf, Bayberry Root Bark, Geranium Root

Diverticulitis

Bowel Cleansing Powder, Marshmallow Root, Licorice Root, Robert's Formula

Flatulence

Fennel Seed, Compounded Elixir of Bitters

Hemorrhoids

Fresh Collinsonia Root, Witch Hazel, Fresh Goldenseal Root, Marshmallow Root, St. Johnswort Oil topically, Comfrey Compound Oil topically

Hemorrhoids – Bleeding

Fresh Collinsonia Root, Fresh Goldenseal Root, Fresh Marshmallow Root, St. Johnswort Oil topically, Comfrey Compound Oil topically

Irritable Bowel Syndrome

Enteric Peppermint Oil, Fresh Marshmallow Root, Bowel Cleansing Powder, Licorice Root, Fresh Goldenseal Root, Robert's Formula

Internal Cleansing Program

One of the great principles of health and healing existing within the system of nature cure is proper elimination. Our physiology is designed with several major eliminative channels: the colon, the kidneys, the lungs, the skin, and the lymphatic system. Invariably, what influences the well-being of each of these systems is the capacity for one's metabolic processes to be carried out correctly. What follows is a brief summary of the herbal blends which, when used together for a period of time, work synergistically to restore balance to the metabolism and digestion and to correct eliminative errors.

Compounded Psyllium Husk, see page 61.
Compounded Elixir of Bitters, see page 84.
Compounded Juniper Berry, see page 51.
Compounded Red Clover, see page 61.

It is suggested that these four herbal compounds within this Internal Cleansing Program be used together for 6 to 8 weeks at the start of each season. During this time it is also suggested that the food intake be lighter, consisting of a higher percentage of whole grains and vegetables. Liquid intake (distilled water and fresh vegetable juice) should be increased. Daily stretching, brisk daily walking, and deep breathing exercises should accompany this program. Also, it would be very beneficial to take some warm water regularly (every 20 minutes) during the day while embarking upon this program.

The results should be noticeable: greater clarity, increased energy, improved digestion and elimination, and a greater sense of well-being.

Mucous Membrane System
Herbal Agents Influencing the Eyes, Ears, Nose, and Throat

Eyes

Cataracts
Herbal eyewash with Rue, Greater Celandine, Dusty Miller, Goldenseal Root, and Eyebright

Conjunctivitis
Eyebright, Fresh Thuja Leaf, Chamomile compresses

Catarrhal Drainage
Compounded Eyebright/Bayberry

Pain
Chamomile compresses

Strain
Gelsemium Root*

*Use only with physician's care.

Ears

Inflammation
Mullein Flower Oil drops, Hypericum Flower Oil drops

Otitis
Mullein Flower Oil drops or Compounded Mullein/
Hypericum Oil drops

Earache
Mullein Flower Oil drops

Tinnitus
Fresh Ginkgo Leaf, Compounded Gotu Kola

Nose

Catarrh
Compounded Eyebright/Bayberry

Sinus Congestion
Compounded Eyebright/Bayberry, Ginger Oil drops

Hay Fever

Compounded Eyebright/Bayberry, Fresh Stinging Nettle Leaf, Compounded Echinacea/Goldenseal, Compounded Turmeric/Catechu

Throat

Laryngitis

Fresh Collinsonia Root, Fresh Horseradish Root, Fresh Goldenseal Root

Pharyngitis

Fresh Red Root, Fresh Horseradish Root

Tonsillitis

Compounded Echinacea/Red Root, Compounded Echinacea/Goldenseal, Fresh Thuja Leaf

Sore Throat

Compounded Echinacea, Compounded Echinacea/Goldenseal (spray on surface tissue), Fresh Collinsonia Root

Mucous Membranes

Catarrh

Compounded Eyebright/Bayberry, Compounded Echinacea

Infections

Compounded Echinacea, Compounded Echinacea/Goldenseal

Vaginitis

Compounded Echinacea/Red Root, Fresh Spilanthes

Tops and Root, Compounded Spilanthes (internally and as douche)

Yeast Infections

Compounded Spilanthes, Compounded Lomatium

Fungal Infections

Compounded Spilanthes, Fresh Spilanthes Tops and Root topically, Fresh Black Walnut Leaf and Hulls

Musculo-Skeletal System
Herbal Agents Influencing the Muscles and Structure

Arthritis

Compounded Red Clover, Compounded Juniper Berry

To these general remedies add the following specifics:

Articular Rheumatoid Arthritis (joints)

Compounded Devil's Claw/Chaparral; Compounded Turmeric/Catechu; Fresh Blue Cohosh Root; compound containing the following herbs: Compounded Yucca/Burdock, Compounded Feverfew/Jamaican Dogwood. Use Compounded Essential Oil Salve topically. For analgesic action, use White Willow Bark.

Muscular Rheumatoid Arthritis (Including Fibrocytis/Myocytis)

Compounded Devil's Claw/Chaparral; Compounded Turmeric/Catechu; Fresh Black Cohosh Root; compound containing the following herbs: Compounded Yucca/Burdock, Compounded Feverfew/Jamaican Dogwood. Use Compounded Essential Oil Salve topically.

Gouty Arthritis

Compounded Devil's Claw/Chaparral, Fresh Pipsissewa Herb, Fresh Juniper Berry, Fresh Burdock Root and Seed, Fresh Stinging Nettle Leaf, Prickly Ash Bark, Compounded Yucca/Burdock. Fresh Ginkgo may be added to assist circulation.

Osteoporosis

Liquid Vitamin K, Alfalfa Solid Extract, Compounded Calcium Elixir, Compounded Elixir of Vitex, Fresh Chaste Tree Extract, Bladderwrack Extract, Compounded Nutritional Elixir

Injuries

Compounded Comfrey Salve or Oil topically, St. Johnswort Oil topically, Arnica and Calendula Flower Oil topically, Compounded Calcium Elixir

Muscular Aches

Compounded Essential Oil Salve topically, Fresh Black Cohosh Root, Lobelia Herb and Seed, Arnica Oil topically, Skullcap, Valerian Root, Compounded Feverfew/Jamaican Dogwood

Nervous System
Herbal Agents Influencing the Nerve Functions

Alzheimer's Disease

Fresh Ginkgo Leaf, Compounded Gotu Kola, Fresh Turmeric Root, Fresh Passionflower

Anxiety

Compounded Elixir of Passionflower, Compounded Skullcap/St. Johnswort, Compounded Melissa

Attention Deficit Disorder

Compounded Melissa, Compounded Elixir of Passionflower, Irish Moss, Kelp

Depression

Fresh St. Johnswort, Fresh Gotu Kola Leaf and Root, Compounded Gotu Kola, Compounded Melissa

Epilepsy

Fresh Black Cohosh, Fresh Passionflower, Fresh Skullcap, Fresh Lobelia Herb and Seed

Headaches

Due to Cold and Flu

Meadowsweet Extract, White Willow Bark Extract, Compounded Feverfew/Jamaican Dogwood

Migraine

Fresh Feverfew Extract, Compounded Feverfew/Jamaican Dogwood, Fresh Ginkgo Leaf

Stress – with Shoulder and Neck Discomfort and Tension

Fresh Black Haw Bark, Jamaican Dogwood, Fresh Skullcap, Fresh Valerian Root, Compounded Feverfew/Jamaican Dogwood

Digestive

Fresh Hops Strobile, Fresh Lavender, Fresh Chamomile, Fresh Black Haw Bark

Hyperactivity

Compounded Melissa, Compounded Elixir of Passionflower

Hysteria

Fresh Skullcap Herb, Compounded Skullcap/St. Johnswort

Insomnia

Compounded Elixir of Passionflower, Compounded Skullcap/St. Johnswort, Fresh Hops Strobile, Fresh Valerian Root

Multiple Sclerosis

Hawthorn Berry Solid Extract, Concentrated Fresh Wild Oats, Compounded Elixir of Passionflower, Compounded Skullcap/St. Johnswort, Compounded Melissa, Fresh Turmeric Root, Fresh Gotu Kola Leaf and Root

Neuralgia

Compounded Feverfew/Jamaican Dogwood, Compounded Skullcap/St. Johnswort, Fresh Valerian Root, Meadowsweet Extract, White Willow Bark Extract

Sciatica

Compounded Skullcap/St. Johnswort, Fresh Valerian Root, Jamaican Dogwood, Meadowsweet Extract

Spasms

Fresh Black Haw Bark, Fresh Black Cohosh Root, Jamaican Dogwood, Fresh Lobelia Herb and Seed, Compounded Feverfew/Jamaican Dogwood

Tinnitis

Fresh Ginkgo Leaf, Compounded Gotu Kola

Reproductive System
Herbal Agents Influencing the Reproductive Functions

Female Reproductive System

Amenorrhea (Absence of Menses)
Compounded Dong Quai, Compounded Elixir of Vitex

Dysmenorrhea (Painful Menstruation)
Compounded Elixir of Vitex, Compounded Dong Quai, Compounded Feverfew/Jamaican Dogwood, Cramp Bark, Black Haw, Jamaican Dogwood

Endometriosis
Compounded Elixir of Vitex, Fresh Chaste Tree Extract, Compounded Dong Quai, Compounded Fraxinus/Ceanothus, Compounded Echinacea/Red Root, Scudder's Alterative

Infertility
Fresh Helonias Root, Fresh Chaste Tree Extract, Chinese Dong Quai Root, Octocossinol

Menopause
Compounded Elixir of Vitex, Fresh Chaste Tree Extract, Alfalfa Solid Extract, Compounded Vitex/Alfalfa

Menorrhagia (Excessive Menstrual Bleeding)
Compounded Dong Quai, Compounded Elixir of Vitex, Fresh Helonias Root, Compounded Echinacea/Red Root, Fresh Goldenseal Root, Fresh Yarrow Flower Extract, Shepherd's Purse Extract, Wild Yam Extract

Ovarian Cysts
Compounded Fraxinus/Ceanothus, Fresh Poke Root,

Fresh Thuja Leaf, Fresh Gelsemium Root*, Scudder's Alterative, Compounded Gelsemium/Phytolacca*

*Use only with physician's care.

Premenstrual Syndrome (PMS)

Compounded Elixir of Vitex, Compounded Dong Quai, Fresh Helonias Root, Evening Primrose Oil

Uterine Fibroids

Compounded Fraxinus/Ceanothus, Compounded Echinacea/Red Root, Fresh Poke Root, Fresh Black Cohosh root, Fresh Gelsemium Root*, Scudder's Alterative

*Use only with physician's care.

Vaginitis

Marshmallow Root and Calendula Flower douche, Compounded Spilanthes internally and as douche

Male Reproductive System

Benign Prostatic Hypertrophy (BPH)

Compounded Saw Palmetto, Fresh Thuja Leaf, Compounded Juniper Berry

Prostate Infection

Compounded Saw Palmetto, Fresh Thuja Leaf, Compounded Echinacea

Prostatitis

Compounded Saw Palmetto, Fresh Thuja Leaf

Respiratory System
Herbal Agents Influencing the Respiratory Functions

Asthma

Compounded Wild Cherry, Compounded Turmeric/Catechu, Chinese Ephedra Extract, Fresh Comfrey Root, Fresh Mullein Extract, Fresh Lobelia Herb and Seed, Fresh Marshmallow Root, Fresh Grindelia Floral Tops

Bronchitis

Fresh Grindelia Floral Tops, Lungwort Extract, Fresh Pleurisy Root, Compounded Echinacea/Goldenseal

Colds

Compounded Echinacea/Goldenseal

Coughs

In all cases use Compounded Wild Cherry with the following specifics:

Dry/Hacking

Yerba Santa, Fresh Sundew Extract, Slippery Elm, Lungwort Extract

Spasmodic

Fresh Sundew Extract, Fresh Lobelia Herb and Seed, Slippery Elm, Marshmallow Extract, Lungwort Extract

Irritative

Yerba Santa Leaf, Fresh Grindelia Floral Buds, Lungwort Extract

Whooping Cough

Fresh Sundew Extract, Fresh Lobelia Herb and Seed, Fresh Red Clover Blossoms

Congestive/Catarrhal

Fresh Eyebright Herb, Fresh Mullein Leaf, Fresh Bloodroot

Croup

Fresh Lobelia Herb and Seed, Fresh Sundew Extract

Emphysema

Cactus grandiflorus Extract, Compounded Bugleweed/ Motherwort, Fresh Lobelia Herb and Seed, Fresh Sundew Extract

Pleurisy

Fresh Pleurisy Root, Fresh Black Cohosh Root, Fresh Stillingia Root, Fresh Lobelia Herb and Seed

Pneumonia

Compounded Echinacea/Goldenseal, Fresh Osha Root, Yerba Santa Leaf, Pleurisy Root, Compounded Lomatium

Skin and Epidermal Tissue
Herbal Agents Influencing the Functions of the Skin

Acne

Oily

Compounded Red Clover, Fresh Yellow Dock Root, Compounded Juniper Berry, Compounded Milk Thistle/ Yellow Dock

With Hormonal Origin

Compounded Red Clover, Sarsaparilla Root

Cystic

Compounded Red Clover, Fresh Burdock Root, Milk Thistle Seed, Compounded Juniper Berry, Compounded Echinacea/Red Root, Compounded Milk Thistle/Yellow Dock, Compounded Scudder's Alterative

Boils/Carbuncles

Fresh Burdock Root, Compounded Red Clover, Compounded Echinacea/Red Root, Compounded Milk Thistle/Yellow Dock, Compounded Scudder's Alterative

Bruises

St. Johnswort Flower Oil topically, Compounded Comfrey Salve, Calendula Flower Oil, Compounded Comfrey Oil

Burns

St. Johnswort Flower Oil topically, Compounded Comfrey Salve, Calendula Flower Oil

Cancer

Compounded Echinacea/Red Root, Fresh Black Walnut Leaf and Hulls, Chaparral Leaf, Fresh Plantain Leaf, Compounded Hoxsey/Red Clover, Compounded Plantain/Goldenseal Salve topically

Dermatitis – Contact

Compounded Comfrey Salve topically

Eczema

Compounded Red Clover, Compounded Juniper Berry, Fresh Burdock Root, Fresh Oregon Grape Root, Compounded

Echinacea, Fresh Thuja Leaf, Compounded Milk Thistle/ Yellow Dock

Herpes Zoster

Compounded Bloodroot/Celandine, Compounded Lomatium, Compounded Skullcap/St. Johnswort, Licorice Root Phytogel, St. Johnswort Extract

Melanomas

Compounded Echinacea/Red Root, Compounded Plantain/ Goldenseal Salve topically, Fresh Turmeric Root, Fresh Thuja Leaf

Shingles

Compounded Skullcap/St. Johnswort, Compounded Lomatium, Compounded Bloodroot/Celandine, Fresh Blue Flag Root

Sores

Fresh Thuja Leaf, Fresh Comfrey Root, Fresh Marshmallow Root, Compounded Echinacea, Compounded Comfrey Salve

Psoriasis

Compounded Red Clover, Compounded Juniper Berry, Fresh Burdock Root, Fresh Oregon Grape Root, Fresh Blue Flag Root, Milk Thistle Seed, Compounded Milk Thistle/Yellow Dock

Warts

Fresh Thuja Leaf Oil topically

Wounds

Fresh St. Johnswort Oil topically, Compounded Comfrey Salve topically

Urinary System
Herbal Agents Influencing the Renal Functions

Bladder Infection

Compounded Usnea/Uva Ursi, Uva Ursi Solid Extract, Buchu Extract

Calculi

Fresh Gravel Root, Bladderwrack Extract, Fresh Marshmallow Root, Compounded Juniper Berry, Madder Root

Cystitis

Fresh Marshmallow Root, Fresh Pipsissewa Herb, Fresh Horsetail Herb, Fresh Corn Silk, Fresh Gravel Root, Compounded Usnea/Uva Ursi, Buchu Extract

Dropsy

Fresh Horsetail Herb, Fresh Wild Carrot, Compounded Juniper Berry, Parsley Tea

Enuresis

Fresh Plantain Leaf, Fresh Thuja Leaf, Fresh St. Johnswort Flower Buds, Fresh Corn Silk,

Gravel

Fresh Marshmallow Root, Fresh Pipsissewa Herb, Compounded Juniper Berry, Bladderwrack Extract, Fresh Gravel Root, Madder Root

Incontinence

Fresh Thuja Leaf, Compounded Juniper Berry, Fresh St. Johnswort Flower Buds, Fresh Corn Silk, Fresh Plantain Leaf, Compounded Plantain/Buchu

Kidney Infection
Compounded Usnea/Uva Ursi, Uva Ursi Solid Extract, Buchu Extract

Kidney Stones
Madder Root, Fresh Gravel Root, Fresh Marshmallow Root

Nephritis
Fresh Goldenrod Flower Tops and Leaf, Fresh Pipsissewa, Fresh Horsetail Herb, Compounded Juniper Berry

Prostatitis
Compounded Saw Palmetto, Fresh Thuja Leaf, Fresh Cleavers Herb, Compounded Echinacea

Suppression
Compounded Juniper Berry, Fresh Goldenrod Flowers and Herb, Fresh Cleavers Herb

Naturopathic Desk Reference

Botanical Therapies for Gynecological Conditions

Gynecological Conditions

Physiology of Hormones
Premenstrual Syndrome
Menopause (estrogen replacement)
Amenorrhea
Dysmenorrhea
Menorrhagia
Ovarian Cysts
Uterine Fibroids
Endometriosis
Fibrocystic Breasts/Mastitis
Infertility
Pregnancy: Herbal Contraindications
   Threatened Miscarriage
   Anemia
   Nausea
   Constipation
   Hemorrhoids
   Urinary Tract Infections
   Hypertension
   Leg Cramps

Botanical Materia Medica

Simple Herbs

Achillea millefolium (Yarrow)
Aletris farinosa (True Unicorn)
Althaea off. (Marshmallow)
Angelica sinesis (Dong Quai)
Arctium lappa (Burdock)
Avena sativa (Oats)
Berberis aquifolium (Oregon Grape)
Capsella bursa-pastoris (Shepherd's Purse)
Caulophyllum thalictroides (Blue Cohosh)
Chamaelirium luteum (False Unicorn/Helonias)
Cimicifuga racemosa (Black Cohosh)
Dioscorea villosa (Wild Yam)
Equisetum arvense (Horsetail)
Glycyrrhiza glabra (Licorice)
Hydrastis canadensis (Goldenseal)
Hyssopus off. (Hyssop)
Leonurus cardiaca (Motherwort)
Medicago sativa (Alfalfa)
Mentha piperita (Peppermint)
Mitchella repens (Squaw Vine)
Phytolacca americana (Poke)
Piscidia erythrina (Jamaican Dogwood)
Pulsatilla spp. (Pulsatilla)
Rumex crispus (Yellow Dock)
Salvia off. (Sage)
Scutellaria lateriflora (Skullcap)
Senicio aureus (Life Root)
Smilax officinalis (Sarsaparilla)
Taraxacum officinalis (Dandelion)
Urtica diocia (Nettles)
Valeriana sitchensis (Valerian)
Viburnum opulus (Cramp Bark)
Viburnum prunifolium (Black Haw)
Zingiber officinalis (Ginger)

Compounds

Compounded Vitamin C Elixir
Compounded Devils Club
Compounded Dong Quai
Compounded Echinacea/Red Root
Compounded Feverfew/Jamaican Dogwood
Compounded Fraxinus/Ceanothus
Compounded Gelsemium/Phytolacca
Compounded Passiflorus Elixir
Compounded Bitters Elixir
Compounded Usnea/Uva Ursi
Compounded Vitex Elixir
Compounded Vitex/Alfalfa

Supplements and Specialty Items

Alfalfa Solid Extract
Bromelain
Calcium
Carotenoids
Castor Oil
Evening Primrose Oil
Lactobacillus
Manganese
Magnesium
Poke Root Oil
Tyrosine
Vitamin B-6
Vitamin K
Flax Seed Oil

The Menstrual Cycle

Menstrual Phase (menstruation): Days 1 to 4

- Estrogen and progesterone withdrawn before onset of menstrual flow.
- Shedding of endometrial lining.

Proliferative (follicular) phase: Days 5 to 14

- Regrowth of endometrial tissue.
- Secretion of follicle-stimulating hormone (FSH) by the pituitary gland.
- Development in ovary of a mature Graafian follicle containing a mature ovum.
- Secretion of increasing amounts of estrogen by Graafian follicle.
- Suppression of FSH when estrogen level becomes high, leading to secretion of luteinizing hormone (LH) by pituitary gland.

The sequence of events in the human menstrual cycle.

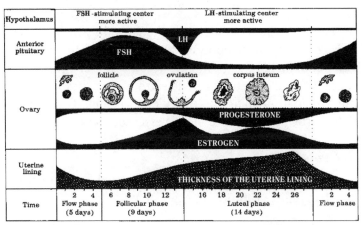

From *Biological Science* by William T. Keeton; illustration by Paula DiSanto Bensadoun.

Secretory (luteal) phase: Days 15 to 25-28

- Rupture of Graafian follicle, releasing ovum (ovulation), starts the secretory phase.
- Movement of ovum through fallopian tube to uterus.
- Formation of corpus luteum at site of ruptured Graafian follicle.
- Production of progesterone by corpus luteum.
- Stimulation by progesterone of endometrial cell growth.
- Significant decrease in progesterone level if implantation does not occur; menstrual phase then begins again.

Oogenesis

There are two ovaries. These produce the female germ cells. The production of ova is a cyclical process called oogenesis.

1. Formation

Germinal epithelium: in development groups of cells migrate into stroma.

2. Growth

Central oogonium enlarges in primordial follicle to become primary oocyte surrounded by follicular cells which multiply to become cumulus oophorus (attaching ovum to wall of follicle) and membrana granulosa which together with cells of theca interna, secrete hormone estrogen, partly stored in liquor folliculi in enlarging cavity of developing Graafian follicle, partly absorbed into blood vessels of theca interna.

3. Ovulation

About 14th day of normal 28-day menstrual cycle, a mature Graafian follicle ruptures to expel ovum.

4. Corpus Luteum

Remaining membrana granulosa and theca interna cells multiply to replace blood clot and secrete hormone progesterone. The corpus luteum shrinks and its output of progesterone falls about the 24th day if fertilization of the shed ovum does not occur. For simplicity the development of only one Graafian follicle is shown here. Several grow in each cycle but in the human subject only one follicle ruptures. The others atrophy, i.e., one mature ovum is shed each month.

Signs and Symptoms of
Premenstrual Syndrome (PMS)

Behavioral

Nervousness, anxiety, and irritability
Mood swings and mild to severe personality changes
Fatigue, lethargy, and depression

Gastrointestinal

Abdominal bloating
Diarrhea and/or constipation
Change in appetite (craving of sugar)

Female

Tender and enlarged breasts
Uterine cramping
Altered libido

General

Headache
Backache
Acne
Edema of fingers and ankles

Hormonal Patterns of Premenstrual Syndrome

- Plasma estrogens are elevated and plasma progesterone levels are reduced 5-10 days before menses
- Prolactin levels are elevated in most PMS women
- Follicle Stimulating Hormone (FSH) levels are elevated 6-9 days prior to the onset of the menses
- Aldosterone levels are marginally elevated 2-8 days prior to the onset of the menses.

Botanical Therapies for Premenstrual Syndrome

PMS-A (Anxiety): *Metabolize Estrogen/Stimulate Progesterone*

Vitex agnus-castus (Chaste Tree Berry)	20-30 drops t.i.d.
Dioscorea villosa (Wild Yam)	30-40 drops t.i.d.
Chamaelirium luteum (Helonias Root)	20-30 drops t.i.d.
Evening Primrose Oil	500 mg q.i.d.
Vitamin B-6	100 mg b.i.d.
Compounded Elixir of Bitters after meals in small amount of water	1 teaspoon
Compounded Elixir of Passionflower	1 teaspoon t.i.d.
Compounded Vitamin C Elixir	1 teaspoon b.i.d.

PMS-C (Cravings): *Promote Digestion/Stimulate Progesterone/Decrease Inflammatory PGE*

Evening Primrose Oil	500 mg q.i.d.
Compounded Bitters Elixir after meals in warm water	1 teaspoon
Compounded Devil's Club	20-30 drops t.i.d.
Angelica sinensis (Dong Quai Root)	30 drops t.i.d.

Taraxacum officinalis
   (Dandelion Root and Leaf)   30-40 drops t.i.d.
Bromelain   500 mg t.i.d.

PMS-D (Depression): Increase Estrogen/Support Adrenals

Compounded Dong Quai	30-40 drops t.i.d.
Glycyrrhiza glabra (Licorice Root)	40 drops t.i.d.
Medicago sativa (Alfalfa Solid Extract)	½ teaspoon t.i.d.
Compounded Elixir of Passionflower	1 teaspoon t.i.d.
Tyrosine	300 mg b.i.d.

PMS-H (Hyperhydration): Balance Hormones/Support Adrenals

Compounded Dong Quai during Follicular phase	30-40 drops t.i.d.
Compounded Elixir of Vitex during luteal Phase	1 teaspoon t.i.d.
Compounded Elixir of Bitters after meals in warm water	1 teaspoon
Glycyrrhiza glabra (Licorice Root)	40 drops t.i.d.
Dioscorea villosa (Wild Yam)	30 drops t.i.d.
Lactobacillus	

Premenstrual Syndrome Sub-Groups

Sub-Group	Symptoms	Mechanics	Prevalence
PMS-A (Anxiety)	Anxiety Irritability Mood Swings Nervous Tension	↑ Estrogen ↓ Progesterone	65-75%
PMS-C (Craving)	Appetite Headache Fatigue Dizziness	↑ Carb. Tolerance ↓ Progesterone ↑ PGEI	24-35%
PMS-D (Depression)	Depression Crying Confusion Forgetfulness	↓ Blood Estrogen ↑ Progesterone ↑ Adrenal	23-37%
PMS-H (Hyper-hydration)	Fluid Retention Weight Gain Breast Tenderness Bloating	↑ Aldosterone	65-72%

Botanical Therapies for Gynecological Conditions

Amenorrhea – Absence of or Delayed Menses

Compounded Dong Quai	30 drops t.i.d.
Compounded Elixir of Vitex	1 teaspoon t.i.d.

Compound of the following herbs:

Caulophylum thalictroides (Blue Cohosh)	20 drops t.i.d.
Chamaelirium luteum (Helonias Root)	20 drops t.i.d.
Senecio aurus (Life Root)	20 drops t.i.d.
Leonurus cardiaca (Motherwort)	20 drops t.i.d.
Zingiber officinalis (Ginger Root)	5 drops t.i.d.
Dioscorea villosa (Wild Yam)	20 drops t.i.d.

Dysmenorrhea – Painful Menstruation

Compounded Dong Quai	30 drops t.i.d.
during Follicular phase	
Compounded Elixir of Vitex	1 teaspoon t.i.d.
during Luteal phase	
Viburnum prunifolium (Black Haw)	30 drops t.i.d.
Caulophylum thalictroides (Blue Cohosh)	20 drops t.i.d.
Piscidia erythrina (Jamaican Dogwood)	30 drops t.i.d.
Scutellaria lateriflora (Skullcap)	30 drops t.i.d.

Note: Take the above 4 single herbs during the onset of menstrual pain. If necessary, take the herbs more often.

Compounded Feverfew/Jamaican Dogwood 40 drops q.i.d.
or more frequently during menstrual pain

Menorrhagia – Excessive or Prolonged Menstrual Bleeding

Compounded Elixir of Vitex	1 teaspoon t.i.d.
Angelica sinensis (Dong Quai Root)	30 drops t.i.d.
Capsella bursa-pastoris (Shepherd's Purse)	40 drops q.i.d.
Achillea millefolium (Yarrow)	20 drops q.i.d.
Hydrastis canadensis (Goldenseal Root)	20 drops t.i.d.

Ovarian Cysts

Scudder's Alterative	30 drops t.i.d.
Compounded Echinacea/Red Root	30-40 drops t.i.d.
Compounded Fraxinus/Ceanothus	30-40 drops q.i.d.
Compounded Gelsemium/Phytolacca	15 drops q.i.d.

Compound the following four herbs:

Taraxacum officinalis (Dandelion Root)	20 drops q.i.d.
Glycyrrhiza glabra (Licorice Root)	20 drops t.i.d.
Rumex crispus (Yellow Dock Root)	20 drops t.i.d.
Arctium lappa (Burdock Root)	20 drops t.i.d.

| Carotenoids: 150,000-300,000 IU | daily |
| Castor Oil Packs over ovaries | 3 to 5 times/week |

If pain is present use:

| *Valeriana sitchensis* (Valerian Root) | 1 teaspoon q.i.d. |
| *Viburnum opulus* (Cramp Bark) | 30 drops t.i.d. |

Uterine Fibroids

Scudder's Alterative	30 drops t.i.d.
Compounded Echinacea/Red Root	30-40 drops t.i.d.
Compounded Fraxinus/Ceanothus	30-40 drops q.i.d.
Compounded Gelsemium/Phytolacca	15 drops q.i.d.
Compounded Vitex Elixir	1 teaspoon t.i.d.
Dong Quai Root	30 drops t.i.d.
Carotenoids: 150,000-300,000 IU	daily

Compound:

Urtica dioica (Nettles)	50 drops t.i.d.
Arctium lappa (Burdock Seed)	20 drops t.i.d.
Taraxacum officinalis (Dandelion Root)	20 drops t.i.d.
Berberis aquifolium (Oregon Grape)	20 drops t.i.d.

Poke Root Oil
    Rub into uterus before bed
Castor Oil packs
    Apply over pelvis 3 to 5 times per week
Sitz baths daily
Herbal Suppositories:
    White Oak Bark
    Goldenseal Root
    Tea Tree Oil

Endometriosis

Scudder's Alterative	30 drops t.i.d.
Compounded Fraxinus/Ceanothus	30-40 drops q.i.d.
Compounded Echinacea/Red Root	30-40 drops t.i.d.

Compounded Vitex Elixir	1 teaspoon t.i.d.
Dong Quai Root	30 drops t.i.d.
Compounded Gelsemium/Phytolacca	15 drops q.i.d.

For Pain:

Compounded Feverfew/Jamaican Dogwood as needed for pain	50-60 drops q.i.d.
Carotenoids: 150,000-300,000 IU	daily
Sitz Baths	daily before bed
Castor Oil Packs over pelvis	3 times/week
Evening Primrose Oil	500 mg q.i.d.

Fibrocystic Breasts/Mastitis

Scudder's Alterative	30 drops t.i.d.
Compounded Echinacea/Red Root	30-40 drops q.i.d.
Phytolacca americana (Poke Root)	10 drops t.i.d.

Compound:

Arctium lappa (Burdock Seed)	20 drops t.i.d.
Taraxacum officinalis (Dandelion Root)	20 drops t.i.d.
Hydrastis canadensis (Goldenseal Root)	20 drops t.i.d.

| Carotenoids: 150,000-300,000 IU | daily |
| Castor Oil/Poke Root Oil Massage | daily |

Mastitis

If breast feeding, apply mullein/lobelia salve to affected area on single breast only, nurse from other breast. Or apply calendula oil to affected breast, nurse from other breast.

Physiology of Menopause

Hypothalamus/Pituitary

These glands are responsible for secretion of FSH and LH hormones (anterior pituitary gonadotrophic hormones). The purpose of FSH and LH hormones is to stimulate the ovaries to produce estrogen.

As the menopause phase begins, ovarian follicles become depleted and less estrogen is secreted. Because of a feedback loop of hormones, there is then less negative feedback on the hypothalamus and women experience and increase in GRH (Gonadotropin Releasing Hormone) and an increase in FSH (Follicle Stimulating Hormone) and a slight increase in LH (Luteinizing Hormone) which in turn attempts to stimulate the ovaries to secrete more estrogen.

At this time ovulation continues even though less estrogen is present. Yet women secrete the same amount of progesterone. The onset of menopause is due to a combination of ovarian aging (depletion of follicles) and extra-ovarian changes.

Depletion of follicles happens at a fairly consistent rate. At the onset of menopause, the rate of depletion accelerates, and because of the feedback loop, increase of FSH hormone (which at one time caused more estrogen to be secreted from ovarian follicles) now is involved in speeding up the depletion of follicles. So, in time, much less estrogen is secreted.

The body may produce more estrogen from sources other than ovaries before menopause and continue after menopause. Adrenals may be involved in estrogen production.

Estrogenic Herbs

Foeniculum vulgare (Fennel)
Salvia off. (Sage)
Cimicifuga racemosa (Black Cohosh)
Angelica sinensis (Dong Quai)
Anisum pimpinella (Anise)
Arctium lappa (Burdock)
Medicago sativa (Alfalfa)
Panax quiqufolia (Ginseng)

Progesterone Herbs

Glycyrrhiza glabra (Licorice)
Smilax off. (Sarsaparilla)
Dioscorea villosa (Wild Yam)

Menopause

Between the ages of 45 and 55 years, ovarian tissues gradually cease to respond to stimulation by anterior pituitary gonadotrophic hormones. After menopause, a woman is unable to bear children.

During and after menopause, the secondary sex organs atrophy. The Fallopian tubes become smaller, while the uterine cycle and menstruation cease. The muscles and lining of the uterus, as well as the vaginal epithelium, reduce in thickness, while the external genitalia shrink.

Ups and downs in emotions are partly related to the fact that the ovaries cease to respond to follicle-stimulating hormone. This results in the reduction of estrogen and progesterone levels in the body. Vasomotor phenomena such as "hot flashes" (vasodilation) can produce excessive sweating and giddiness. The ovary becomes small and fibrosed, and no longer produces ripe ova. There can also be a reversal of typically female secondary sex characteristics: body fat may be redistributed, the breasts may shrink along with the internal ducts, and hair may become sparse in the axillary area (armpit) and the pubis.

Estrogen Replacement Therapy

Basic Estrogen Replacement

Medicago sativa (Alfalfa Solid Extract)	1 teaspoon b.i.d.
Compounded Vitex Elixir	1 teaspoon t.i.d.
Compounded Vitex/Alfalfa	30-40 drops q.i.d.

If symptomatology is present, compound the following herbs:

Caulophylum thalictroides (Blue Cohosh)	20 drops t.i.d.
Hyssopus officinalis (Hyssop)	20 drops t.i.d.
Scutellaria lateriflora (Skullcap)	20 drops t.i.d.
Salvia officinalis (Sage)	20 drops t.i.d.
Chamaelirium luteum (Helonias Root)	20 drops t.i.d.
Glycyrrhiza glabra (Licorice Root)	10 drops t.i.d.
Arctium lappa (Burdock Root)	20 drops t.i.d.
Dioscorea villosa (Wild Yam)	30 drops t.i.d.
Evening Primrose Oil	500 mg. t.i.d.

Take the above program for 4 to 6 months, then take 1 month off before continuing for another 4 to 6 months.

Specific Differentiation:

Vitex agnus castus (Chaste Tree berry)	30 drops t.i.d.
Chelidonium major (Greater Celandine)	10 drops t.i.d.
Cimicifuga racemosa (Black Cohosh)	15 drops t.i.d.
Pulsatilla spp.	5 drops t.i.d.

The above compound is to be taken when there is lability and nervous over-excitability.

Menopause Differentiation

The following differentiations are added to the standard botanical estrogen replacement therapy cited above.

Hot Flashes

Compound:

Salvia officinalis (Sage)	20 drops
Leonurus cardiaca (Motherwort)	20 drops
Mentha piperita (Peppermint)	20 drops
Compounded Vitex/Alfalfa	40 drops q.i.d.

Osteoporosis

Avena sativa (Wild Oats)

Urtica dioica (Nettles)
Althaea officinalis (Marshmallow Root)
Rumex crispus (Yellow Dock)
Equisetum officinalis (Horsetail)

Drink 3 cups daily using liberal amounts of herbs to make strong decoction.

Manganese	2.5 mg/day
Liquid Vitamin K	5 mg/day

Blood Sugar Changes

Compounded Devil's Club	30-40 drops q.i.d.
Arctium lappa (Burdock Root)	30 drops q.i.d.
Glycyrrhiza glabra (Licorice Root)	20 drops t.i.d.

Genito-Urinay

Compounded Usnea/Uva Ursi (if UTI present) or more frequently	30-60 q.i.d.
Compound:	
Helonias Root (False Unicorn)	20 drops t.i.d.
Smilax officinalis (Sarsaparilla)	20 drops t.i.d.
Aletris (True Unicorn)	20 drops t.i.d.

Infertility

Compound of the following herbs:

Chamelirium luteum (Helonias Root)	30 drops t.i.d.
Vitex agnus-castus (Chaste Tree Berry)	20 drops t.i.d.
Mitchella repens (Squaw Vine)	20 drops t.i.d.
Aletris farinosa (True Unicorn)	15 drops t.i.d.
Lobelia incarnata (Lobelia)	10 drops t.i.d.
Zingiber officinalis (Ginger Root)	10 drops t.i.d.

Octocossinol	500 mg q.i.d.
Wheat Germ Oil	1 teaspoon b.i.d.

Tea prepared of the following herbs:
Urtica dioica (Nettles)
Avena sativa (Oat seed/straw)
Rubus idaeus (Raspberry leaf)

Take large amount of each herb (1 handful) and add to 2 quarts boiling water. Simmer on low for 20 minutes, turn off heat and steep overnight. In morning, strain and warm, then add 1 tablespoon He Sho Wu Tonic. Drink 1 quart

Pregnancy

Three Stages in a Cycle Ending in Pregnancy

The fimbriated end of the uterine tube receives ovum at ovulation. The uterine tube also transmits spermatozoa towards the ova.

1. **Fertilization**. Fusion of ovum and sperm occurs in outer third of uterine tube.

2. **Cleavage**. After fertilization in Fallopian tube, the fertilized ovum (zygote) undergoes several divisions. Ciliary currents and penstaltic contractions in Fallopian tube carry blastocyst into uterine secretions around the fourth to the seventh day.

3. **Implantation**. For a few days, the embryo gets oxygen and nutrients by diffusion from the uterine glandular secretions. The embryo sticks to lining of womb. Its surface trophoblast cells fuse with, destroy, and finally penetrate the endometrium (now called the desidua). The embryo now absorbs tissue fluids and cellular debris. Chorionic villi, finger-like projections from the embryo, invade the mother's endometrial blood vessels. The endometrium is in luteal phase, and continues to grow. No menstrual degeneration occurs. Glands are actively secreting mucus.

Herbs Contraindicated During Pregnancy

By Actions:
- (US) Uterine Stimulants
- (E) Emmenogogues
- (A) Abortifacients

By Chemistry:
- (AL) Anthraquinone Laxatives
- (EO) Essential Oils
- (AK) Alkaloids
- (B) Bitter Principles

Achillea millefolium (Yarrow)	EO, B, E
Acorus calamus (Calamus)	B, E, US
Artemisia spp. (Wormwood)	US, E, A, EO
Berberis vulgaris (Barberry)	B, AK
Capsicum spp. (Cayenne)	EO, US
Chelidonium majus (Celandine)	AK, B
Dryopteris filix-mas (Male fem)	B, US
Ephedra spp. (Ephedra)	AK, B
Foeniculum vulgare (Fennel)	EO, US
Glycyrrhiza glabra (Licorice)	US, E
Hydrastis canadensis (Goldenseal)	B, AK, US
Juniperus communis (Juniper)	EO, B
Lavandula officinalis (Lavender)	EO, B
Linum usitatissimum (Flaxseed)	US
Mentha pulegium (Pennyroyal)	EO, US, E, A
Passiflora incarnata (Passion Flower)	EO, US, E
Phytolacca americana (Poke Root)	US, E, A
Podophyllum peltatum (Mayapple)	US, E, A, AL
Prunus serotina (Wild Cherry)	B, US
Rhamnus spp. (Cascara Sagrada)	E, US, AL,
Rheum spp. (Rhubarb)	E, US, AL B
Salvia officinalis (Sage)	EO, B, US
Sanguinara canadensis (Bloodroot)	AK, P, US

Tanacetum vulgare (Tansy)	EO, B, US, E, A
Thuja occidentalis (Thuja)	EO, US, E
Thymus vulgaris (Thyme)	EO, US, E
Vinca rosea (Periwinkle)	US, E
Viscum album (Mistletoe)	US, E

Herbs to be Used with Caution During Pregnancy

Angelica archangelica (Angelica)
Angelica sinensis (Dong Quai)
Arctium lappa (Burdock)
Arctostaphylos uva ursi (Uva Ursi)
Calendula officinalis (Calendula)
Centella asiatica (Gotu Kola)
Hypericum perforatum (St. Johnswort)
Hyssopus officinalis (Hyssop)
Leonurus cardiaca (Motherwort)
Marrubium vulgare (Horehound)
Matricaria chamomilla (German Chamomile)
Medicago sativa (Alfalfa)
Melissa officinalis (Lemon Balm)
Mentha piperita (Peppermint)
Plantago spp. (Plantain)
Silybum marianum (Milk Thistle)
Tanacetum parthenium (Feverfew)
Trigonella foenum-graecum (Fenugreek)
Urtica dioica (Nettles)
Zingiber officinalis (Ginger)

Useful Herbs During Pregnancy

Caulophyllum thalictroides (Blue Cohosh)*
Chamaelirium luteum (Helonias/False Unicorn)
Crataegus spp. (Hawthorn)
Dioscorea villosa (Wild Yam)

Mitchella repens (Squaw Vine)
Rubus idaeus (Red Raspberry)
Scutellaria lateriflora (Skullcap)
Taraxacum officinalis (Dandelion)
Urtica dioica (Nettles)
Viburnum opulus (Cramp Bark)
Viburnum prunifolium (Black Haw)

*During Last Trimester Only

Botanical Therapies for Conditions During Pregnancy

Threatened Miscarriage

Compound:

Viburnum prunfolium (Black Haw)	20-30 drops q.i.d.
Chamaelirium luteum (Helonias Root)	20-30 drops q.i.d.
Cimicifuga racemosa (Black Cohosh)	20-30 drops q.i.d.
Viburnum opulus (Cramp Bark)	20-30 drops q.i.d.

Anemia

Decoction (tea) of the following herbs:
 Rubus idaeus (Red Raspberry Leaf)
 Taraxacum officinalis (Dandelion Root)
 Urtica dioica (Nettles)
 Avena sativa (Oats)
 Rumex crispus (Yellow Dock)

Drink 16-24 oz. per day of the above tea

Yellow Dock Extract	30 drops t.i.d.
Compounded Nutritional Elixir	1 tsp. b.i.d./t.i.d.
Chlorella algae	1 teaspoon b.i.d.
in water	
Folic Acid	

Nausea

Gentiana Lutea (Gentian)	20 drops t.i.d.
Filipendula ulmaria (Meadowsweet)	20 drops t.i.d.
Foeniculum vulgare (Fennel)	20 drops t.i.d.
Cinnamonum aromaticum (Cinnamon)	20 drops t.i.d.
Zingiber officinalis (Ginger)	5 drops t.i.d.
Liquid Vitamin K	5 mg/day

Constipation

• Stewed Figs. Simmer 10 figs in 16 oz. water for 10 minutes. Steep overnight. In the morning, drink warm fig juice and eat figs throughout the day.

• Oat Milk. Soak freshly ground oats in water overnight, 3 pounds water to 1 pound oats. In the morning, strain through cheesecloth, saving milk of oats. Warm oat milk and add fig juice or prune juice to sweeten. Also add 30 drops *Glycyrrhiza glabra* (Licorice Extract) to oat milk.

• Pure Extra Virgin Olive Oil: Take 1 Tablespoon 3 times daily, between meals.

• Do yoga stretching exercises/abdominal stretches daily.

Compound:

Rumex crispus (Yellow Dock)	15 drops t.i.d.
Taraxacum officinalis (Dandelion Root)	15 drops t.i.d.
Dioscorea villosa (Wild Yam)	10 drops t.i.d.
Ulmus rubra (Slippery Elm)	½-1 tsp. t.i.d.
Pimpinella anisum (Anise)	10 drops t.i.d.

Add the above mixture to Compounded Psyllium Husk Powder. Take 1 teaspoon in large glass of warm water. Add herbal extracts above and take once a day.

Hemorrhoids

• Rub or inject with a small syringe into rectum Comfrey Compounded Oil b.i.d.

• Take warm sitz baths each evening before bed for 15 to 20 minutes.

Urinary Tract Infections (UTI)

Compounded Usnea/Uva Ursi   40-60 drops
    every 2 hours or until infection subsides.

Note: Do not drink cranberry juice at this time.

Hypertension

Compound:

Crataegus (Hawthorn Supreme)	40-60 drops q.i.d.
Taraxacum (Dandelion Root/Leaf)	20-30 drops q.i.d.
Tilia spp. (Linden)	20 drops q.i.d.
Matricaria chamomilla (Chamomile)	20 drops q.i.d.

Drink warm water every 15 minutes throughout the day.

Leg Cramps

Compounded Calcium Elixir	1 teaspoon b.i.d.
when cramps appear	
Viburnum opulus (Cramp Bark)	20 drops
Viburnum prunfolium (Black Haw)	20 drops

Take the above herbs t.i.d. when cramps appear.

Botanical Therapies for Disorders of Immediate-type Hypersensitivity

Disorders of Immediate-Type Hypersensitivity

Asthmatic Reactions
Allergies
Hives
Urticaria
Reactive Dermatitis
Reactive Inflammatory Arthritis
Reactive Psoriasis
Irritable Bowel Syndrome

Botanical Materia Medica

Achillea millefolium (Yarrow)
Angelica sinensis (Dong Quai)
Catechu nigrum (Black Catechu)
Camellia thea (Green Tea)
Curcuma longa (Turmeric)
Echinacea spp. (Echinacea)
Ephedra sinensis (Ma Huang)
Euphrasia off. (Eyebright)
Ginkgo biloba (Ginkgo)
Glycyrrhiza glabra (Licorice)
Grindelia robusta (Grindelia)
Harpagophytum procumbens (Devil's Claw)
Hydrastis canadensis (Goldenseal)
Lobelia inflata (Lobelia)
Myrica cerifera (Bayberry)
Silybum marianum (Milk Thistle)
Urtica dioica (Stinging Nettles)

The Allergic Response Syndrome

The allergy syndrome, now being referred to medically as disorders of immediate type hypersensitivity includes a broad spectrum of health imbalances which include asthma, allergies (pollen, animal dander, molds, airborne pollutants, etc.), hives, urticaria, reactive dermatitis, food allergies, psoriasis, reactive inflammatory arthritis, irritable bowel syndrome, spastic colon, colitis anaphylaxis shock syndrome, etc. Primary sites of reactivity include the skin, mucous membranes, and joints. The reactivities occur as a result of a hypersensitivity and instability of the secretory immune system which partly consists of the mucous membrane throughout the body.

Imbedded in these tissues are immune cells called mast cells which become unstable and eventually degranulate when they are repeatedly contacted by allergens originating either from the environment or as a byproduct of metabolism. Eventually inflammatory histamines and other inflammatory substances "leak" through the membranes, evoking the inflammatory response. Mucous membranes may become irritated and swollen and secrete excess mucous. Skin may become irritated, itchy, and develop hives or urticaria or break out in psoriatic lesions. Joints may become painful and inflamed. Bowels may become irritated and spastic, with resulting malabsorption. All of the above reactivities occur as a result of pathways of inflammation becoming activated through the release of inflammatory substances from mast cells.

Food Allergies

Cytotoxic Reactions

Tissue injury occurs when IgG or IgM antibodies bind to cell-bound antigens. Antigen-antibody binding can eventually cause cell destruction where the antigen is bound.

Immune Complex-Mediated Reactions

Resulting tissue injury is due to binding of antigens to antibodies, which eventually deposit in tissues. These reactions result from circulating antigenic complexes and vasoactive amines found in food.

The resolution of this immediate type of hypersensitivity and food allergies includes the following approaches:

- Stabilize mast cells
- Improve mucous membrane integrity
- Improve integrity of gut and intestinal mucosa
- Enhance the adrenal response towards the activation of inflammatory pathways
- Protect liver integrity and improve the ability of the liver to clear these allergens from the system
- Provide immune support

The botanical approach to this resolution includes largely the use of flavonoids derived from many specific plants. Four important flavonoids (quercetin, curcumin, catechin, and silymarin) are derived from the use of the following plants: Turmeric root, Catechu, and Milk Thistle seed. These plants significantly improve mast cell and mucous membrane integrity and protect hepatocytes, while improving the ability of the liver to clear antigens from the system. The following botanical protocol has been developed as a thorough treatment for all disorders of immediate type hypersensitivity.

Botanical Therapy for
Immediate-Type Hypersensitivity Disorder

Compounded Turmeric/Catechu   30-40 drops
   3 to 4 times daily between meals for 4 to 6 months

Fresh Nettles Extract   30-50 drops
   3 to 4 times daily 1 month prior to onset of allergy season
   and continue for 4 to 6 months
Compounded Echinacea   30-40 drops q.i.d.
Licorice Root Solid Extract   ⅛-¼ teaspoon
   2 times daily for 2 to 4 weeks
Compounded Bitters Elixir   ½-1 teaspoon
   3 times daily in a small amount of warm water before
   meals for 4 to 6 months
Compounded Psyllium Husk Powder   1 heaping tsp.
   in a full glass of warm water 2 times daily for 3 to 4
   months
Compounded Vitamin C Elixir   1 tsp. b.i.d.
Linseed Oil   1 Tbs. b.i.d.

Differentiations

Compounded Eyebright/Bayberry   20-30 drops
   3 times daily for 2 weeks

NOTE: To be used only if allergic response includes excessive
mucous secretions and exudations

Ma Huang   30-40 drops
   3 to 4 times daily for 2 weeks

NOTE: To be used only if bronchial constriction is present

Compound for Asthma

   Grindelia robusta (Grindelia)   30 drops q.i.d.
   Glycyrrhiza glabra (Licorice)   20 drops q.i.d.
   Lobelia inflata (Lobelia)   10 drops q.i.d.
   Compounded Vitamin C Elixir   ½ teaspoon q.i.d.

Add the above to warm water or Green tea

Green tea   2-4 cups daily

Compounded Turmeric/Catechu

Curcuma longa (Turmeric)
Catechu nigra (Black Catechu)
Grindelia robusta (Grindelia)
Glycyrrhiza glabra (Licorice)
Rosa rugosa (Rose Hips)
Scutellaria baicalensis (Chinese Skullcap)
Ginkgo biloba (Ginkgo)
Harpagophytum procumberis (Devil's Claw)
Achillea millefolium (Yarrow)
Lobelia inflata (Lobelia)

Compounded Eyebright/Bayberry

Euphrasia off. (Eyebright)
Myrica cerfera (Bayberry)
Hydrastis canadensis (Goldenseal)
Acorus calamus (Calamus)
Urtica dioica (Nettles)

Compounded Bitters Elixir

Curcuma longa (Turmeric)
Emblica off. (Indian Gooseberry)
Silybum marianum (Milk Thistle)
Dioscorea villosa (Wild Yam)
Gentiana lutea (Gentian)
Acorus calamus (Calamus)
Foeniculum vulgare (Fennel)
Elettaria cardimomum (Cardamon)

Compounded Psyllium Husk Powder

Plantago ovata (Psyllium)
Triphala concentrate
Althaea off. (Marshmallow)
Glycyrrhiza glabra (Licorice)
Zingiber off. (Ginger)

Stress, Adaptogens, and the Immune System

Harmonizing the Chemistry of Man with the Chemistry of Nature

A study of the teaching and writing of some of the most respected physicians, teachers, and practitioners of natural methods of healing reveals the following five principals of nature cure:

> Nerve Integrity
> Blood and Lymphatic Integrity
> Circulation
> Assimilation
> Elimination

These five fundamental principals of health, if operating in a balanced way within the physiology, will result in the improvement of the vital force of the individual.

Nerve Integrity

To have healthy nerve integrity is to have a strong and balanced nerve system, nerve cells, nerve sheath, brain cells, and spinal cord. All information and electrical impulses are coordinated and carried out through the nerve system network. The nerve system is supported and maintained nutritionally by several fundamental elementals, which include calcium, magnesium, sodium, potassium, phosphorus, silicon, iron, and iodine. The elemental forms of these minerals as they occur naturally in the vegetative and animal kingdom carry the wisdom of nature's intelligence so that they target and align to the designated complementary receptors in the body.

Calcium: "The Great Builder"

Calcium and its elemental forms such as calcium phosphate,

calcium chloride, and calcium fluoride are essential for healthy nerve, brain, and structural integrity. With elemental calcium, new tissues and cells remain strong and vital. Calcium maintains the connective network within the body and supports the solidarity of the body. Elemental forms of calcium in foods and herbs are best found in seeds such as sesame, sunflower, and pumpkin, as well as almonds, figs, dark greens, oats, rice, barley, carrots, and seaweeds. Excellent herbal sources of elemental calcium are oats, horsetail, skullcap, hawthorn berry, gotu kola, and stinging nettles.

Magnesium: "The Great Relaxer"

Magnesium in its elemental form as it naturally occurs in plants is considered to be the finest relaxer, tranquilizer, and laxative in nature. Magnesium brings relaxation to an agitated nerve system and soothes irritation to the tissues and cells associated with nerve function. It also relieves constipation and irritation to the bowels, resulting from an over-stressed physiology. Elemental forms of magnesium in foods and herbs are best found in many orange and yellow foods such as carrots, yellow squash, sweet potato, and yellow corn, as well as black mission figs, and raw goat's milk. Herbal sources of magnesium include gotu kola, skullcap, horsetail, alfalfa, nettles, hawthorn berry, and wild oat seed.

Sodium: "The Youth Element"

Sodium in its naturally occurring form is considered to bring youthfulness to the body's tissues, membrane linings, and joints. Sodium is essential for healthy digestion and supple capillaries and arteries. It is necessary to maintain flexibility and mobility in the joints. Without proper sodium the joints would stiffen and calcify prematurely. Without proper sodium the lining of the stomach would not secrete the necessary enzymes for healthy digestion.

The sun is considered the sodium star, so all fruits and

vegetables which are ripened by the sun contain ample amounts of sodium. Other significant sources of sodium include seaweed such as kelp, dulse, and nori, as well as black mission figs, whey, celery, and raw goat milk. Herbal sources of sodium include alfalfa, chlorella, spirulina, stinging nettles, and raspberry leaf.

Potassium: "The Great Alkalizer"

Potassium salts as they occur naturally in foods bring alkalinity to the blood chemistry. Potassium neutralizes acids in blood chemistry which build from incorrect metabolism of unsuitable foods for the constitution. Potassium, when in balance, prevents the growth of cysts, fibroids, and other benign growths. Without potassium balance, the nervous system may become agitated, thoughts become disturbed and the entire psycho-physiological balance is upset. All fresh fruits and vegetables contain ample amounts of potassium, especially figs, celery, dandelion greens, and other dark green leafy vegetables. Herbal sources of potassium include stinging nettles, dandelion, alfalfa, seaweed, parsley, and chickweed.

Phosphorus: "The Light Bearer"

Phosphorus feeds both the brain and nerve cells as well as the bones. Brain and nerve phosphorus is obtained largely through animal derivatives and single cell algae, while bone phosphorus can be obtained through seeds and nuts. Without adequate phosphorus to feed the constitution, one may feel dull and lethargic and may lack radiance. One's bones may be deficient and early structural disorders may arise. A vegetarian must maintain spiritual and emotional balance in order to hold adequate phosphorus in the system. Sources of phosphorus derived from fish and poultry, seeds, nuts, and whole grains can adequately keep balance in the physiology.

Silicon: "The Magnetic Element"

Silicon in its naturally occurring form feeds the nerve cells, nerve sheath, hair, nails, skin, eyes, teeth, brain cells, and tissues. Silica brings magnetism to the nerves, radiance to the skin, and luster to the hair, builds strong teeth and nails, and brings balance to the emotional system. A person lacking silica will be tense, irritable, rough, appear cold and difficult to get to know, lack luster, and generally feels on edge much of the time. A person rich in silica will sparkle, radiate joy and harmony, express dynamism in personality, attract others, show luster in hair, eyes, teeth, and nails, and generally be very magnetic. People are naturally drawn to silica-rich people. Without adequate silica, one remains lonely and feels depleted. Silica is naturally found in the outer husks of whole grains, seeds, and nuts. Rich herbal sources of silica include horsetail, wild oats, dandelion leaf, onions, alfalfa, and stinging nettles.

Iron: "The Frisky Horse Element"

Iron is the element which builds vigor and stamina into the constitution. Iron gives strength and virility. Without adequate iron the blood becomes depleted and one feels weak, anemic, and frail. Iron from inorganic sources may not be absorbed well into the tissues and can cause constipation, yeast overgrowth, and can lead to auto-intoxication. Iron attracts oxygen into the constitution and gives mental energy and clarity of mind. Naturally occurring sources of iron are figs, raisins, dark green leafy vegetables, black cherries, chlorella, spirulina, stinging nettles, dandelion leaf, raspberry leaf, alfalfa, chickweed, parsley, and red clover. Herbal iron tonics, inclusive of the herbs, are best assimilated when gentian root is added to the formula – due to its nascent oxygen which aids in the assimilation of iron.

Iodine: "The Emotional Metabolizer Element"

Iodine is the element which feeds the thyroid gland and maintains metabolic and emotional balance throughout the body. Without adequate iodine, the thyroid gland may become dysfunctional and lead to metabolic changes. Every emotion which we experience is processed through the thyroid gland. Without adequate iodine, emotional instability may arise and the nervous system may feel distraught. Ample sources of iodine are found in seaweeds such as kelp, dulse, and nori, as well as onions and black walnut hulls and nuts.

Each of the preceding chemical elements is intimately connected to healthy nerve integrity in its own way. When the body is in chemical balance, the nerve cells and tissues maintain sufficient vitality to eliminate metabolic wastes and to coordinate all electrical and nerve impulses throughout the system.

Blood and Lymphatic Integrity

The two main bodily fluids, the blood and lymph, require proper chemical and metabolic balance. When the blood and lymph fluids are laden with toxic wastes, other organ and tissue functions become impeded. One simple nature cure method of maintaining healthy blood and lymph fluids is to drink regular warm water throughout the day. Warm water keeps the body's channels open, permitting vital energy to flow through the system. Warm water also enables wastes to soften and loosen from impacted areas so that they may be eliminated freely. Warm water also enables toxins to be flushed out of the system throughout the day so that one's energy may be sustained evenly.

Another nature cure method to enhance blood and lymphatic integrity is to do regular morning dry skin brushing upon rising. Dry skin brushing invigorates the peripheral circulation and mobilizes toxic lymph to drain into eliminative channels for better elimination. Alterative herbal therapies, which alter processes of waste and nutrition through metabolism, are effective in enhancing blood and lymphatic integrity. Some effective alterative therapies include Scudder's Alterative Compound, Compounded Red Clover, Compounded Hoxsey/Red Clover, and Compounded Echinacea/Red Root. (See "The Dispensatory Guide to the Use of Herbal Compounds" for specific information on these alterative therapies.)

Circulation

All nutrients are carried through the system within the circulatory system. To feed the cells and tissues properly, the organs of circulation – the heart, lungs, and spleen – must be functioning healthfully. Fresh, clean air, exercise, and deep breathing exercises promote healthy circulation. Constitutional herbal therapies which promote healthy circulation include Compounded Hawthorn, ginkgo leaf, ginger root, prickly ash bark, cayenne pepper, Siberian ginseng, as well as the herbs cited above.

Assimilation

Real assimilation begins when the sun's influence comes in contact with the body at dawn. The sun is the fire element in nature and as it grows stronger in the sky, it builds the fires of appetite and digestion. When the sun is highest in the sky, digestion and assimilation are at their strongest. Therefore, it makes sense naturopathically to eat one's largest meal during the noon hour.

Some people believe that "you are what you eat." This is perhaps only a partial truth. What may be more truthful is "you are what you assimilate." Eastern medicine (Ayurvedic and

Chinese) is founded on the premise that health is born of strong digestion.

Another value of assimilation is born of our experiences. Every experience that we entertain – every thought, every like and dislike, every instinct, every emotion, literally every impulse of the breath of life – gets assimilated into our psychophysiology and creates our physical body. Our body is the endproduct of our experiences. Daily experiences get metabolized and transmuted into physical matter. Therefore it is essential to cultivate healthy assimilation of our daily life by creating routines which are in balance with the operating principles and forces of nature.

Elimination

We find that if the previous four principles of nature cure are attended to properly and routinely, the byproduct will be healthy elimination through all the eliminative channels. There are six major channels of elimination: the skin, kidneys, bowel, liver, lungs, and lymph. With a healthy routine, fresh air, clean water, healthy foods, graceful eating of food, exercise, and life-supporting environments, all channels of elimination should be impacted favorably. It should not be necessary to resort to laxatives of any kind to move one's bowels. Constipation results from improper digestion and improper maintenance of nerve force.

When all five principles of nature cure are operating freely and routinely, the most fundamental result will be the revitalization of the vital force within the body.

Formula for Vitality
Restoration of the Vital Force

Power and vitality result from the elimination of obstructing wastes in the body and secondly from assimilating "nature" into the physiology. Vital force is the key ingredient for health and longevity. All physio-medical therapy attempts to restore the vital force. When vital force is strong, immunity is strong. In Ayurvedic medicine, it is said that when digestion is at its peak, then "*ojas*" is produced as the most refined substance of digestion. *Ojas* is the nectar of life it sustains life. When *ojas* is strong then one gets "*bala.*" *Bala* is an Ayurvedic term which is translated to mean strength and immunity. From this perspective it is clear that digestion is of key importance for vital force, which is of key importance for immunity from disease.

The Adaptive Syndrome

Adaptogenic Medicine: Strengthening the Powers of Resistance

The term "adaptogenic medicine" was first coined by a Russian scientist, Lazarev, who referred to medically-effective substances which he called adaptogens as substances which put the body into a state of nonspecific heightened resistance in order to better resist stress and adapt to extraordinary challenges. Dr. Hans Selye, a Swedish scientist who won a Nobel Prize for his work on stress, formulated what he called the General Adaptive Syndrome. It was Selye who said that there is no stressful situation in life, only a stressful response. How we respond to stress determines the effect that stress will have on us.

Selye felt the limiting factor which determined our adaptive capacity and resulting immunity was what he coined the "Adaptations Energy" of the body. He felt that one's powers of resistance and resistance reserves are not inexhaustible, and that they diminish when the body is continuously exposed to extreme stress, the consequences being misadaptation, lowered immunity, and the onset of disease.

Selye's General Adaptive Syndrome provided for three distinct phases:

1. The "Alarm Reaction"

This is the first phase, which is a response to the exposure to stressful stimuli. This phase sets in usually within a few minutes to several hours after exposure to the stress. Sympathetic nerve changes occur which represent the body's response to stress; generally, the body begins a degenerative process which invariably raises the nonspecific resistance capacity.

2. The "Stage of Resistance"

If the stressor prevails upon the body, the second phase sets in. The body may respond with a heightened capacity of resistance to the stressor. In this phase the Adaptive Energy is sufficient enough to bring about a normalization of the changes which originated during the first phase. Here the body becomes increasingly resistant until optimal adaptation is achieved.

3. The "Stage of Exhaustion"

If the stressor is permitted to expose the body and goes beyond a certain limit, the "Adaptive Energy" becomes depleted. Here the resistance of the body is exhausted. The capacity for adaptation is lost. In this phase the organs and cells and tissues begin to break down and eventually disease begins to set in.

Naturally, one would want to recognize the impact of a stressor and change the environment so that the powers of resistance remain strong. A Russian scientist, Brekhman, coined the term "Adaptogenic Medicine" recognizing that there were substances in nature which could sustain the powers of resistance when stressors continue to expose the body. Brekhman saw that in the plant kingdom there were specific plants which had the capacity to exert an "Adaptogenic Effect" upon the physiology. He referred to these plants as adaptogens. He summarized the concept of plant adaptogens in the following way:

1. The plant must show a nonspecific effect (raising the powers of resistance to stressors of a physical, chemical, or emotional nature).
2. The plant must normalize the physiology; it must restore balance and equilibrium even in the presence of pathological conditions.
3. The plant must be nontoxic and harmless to any organ or tissue within the body.

Thus adaptogens are plant substances capable of strengthening the nonspecific powers of resistance to stress, capable of raising the general performance capacity during stressful exposure, and capable of preventing disease which may develop due to over-stressing the body.

Herbs Known for their Adaptogenic Effects

Siberian Ginseng (Eleutherococcus senticosus)

This plant contains compounds known as eleutherosides which are primarily responsible for the adaptogenic attributes which it exhibits. There also exists immunomodulating polysaccharides (long-chain sugar molecules) found in the root. Studies show that, when taken regularly, the adaptogenic effects of Siberian Ginseng permit a greater resistance to adverse conditions such as excessive workload and exercise, exposure to pollutants, exposure to excessive noise and environmental stress, and stress due to pathogenesis, including cancer, arthritis, diabetes, hypertension, heart disease, respiratory disorders, nerve disorders, as well as a variety of other ailments. Although Siberian Ginseng may not be a cure for any of these pathogenic conditions, it has been shown to bring more balance and equilibrium to the physiology when affected by these ailments. Generally, Siberian Ginseng is found useful for anyone undergoing a stress overload and seems to be more effective if taken cumulatively over a period of 4 to 6 months. Generally if taken over this time Siberian Ginseng will exhibit marked anti-stress effects, endocrine effects (lowers cholesterol, increases corticosteroids, increases secretions of male reproductive glands), and anabolic effects (improves protein synthesis in liver, pancreas, and adrenal cortex).

American Ginseng (Panax quinquifolius)

This plant contains a group of saponin compounds known as ginsenosides. Ginsenosides in the roots of American Ginseng have been shown to have an adaptogenic effect similar to that of Siberian Ginseng. The general adaptive energies of the body are strengthened, bringing a greater resistance to stressful stimuli. American Ginseng has also been shown to exhibit anti-tumor, anti-viral, antioxidant, metabolic, and endocrine properties. It has been shown to reduce fatigue, strengthen adrenal response, enhance reproductive performance, improve liver metabolism, and enhance immunity. The Chinese regard American Ginseng as a yin tonic, reducing heat in the digestive and respiratory systems. For this reason it is considered more favorable for individuals with a hotter constitution.

Schizandra Berry (Schizandra chinensis)

Schizandra Berries originate in China and are considered to possess general adaptogen activity, regulating a variety of body functions and improving the body's response to stress.

Schizandra exhibits three ranges of actions. Firstly, it shows marked anti-hepatotoxic and hepatoprotective action. In this respect it protects liver cells, promotes regeneration of hepatocytes, enhances liver detoxification, and is effective in the treatment of chronic hepatitis and cirrhosis. Secondly, it shows marked metabolic action, increasing hepatic glycogen content and relieving fatty degeneration of the liver. Thirdly, its adaptogenic action is strong in improving overall response to stress, improving sensory response, and strengthening central and peripheral nerve systems.

Ashwagandha Root (Withania somnifera)

In Ayurvedic medicine the root is said to "protect the organism from illness through maintaining the healthy balance of physical energies." It is considered to be a tonic in a similar sense as that of Ginseng. Like other adaptogens, Ashwagandha exhibits an anti-stress effect, an immunomodulatory effect, it enhances both short- and long-term memory, and exhibits antiinflammatory properties.

Astragalus Root (Astragalus membranaceus)

In Chinese medicine, Astragalus is considered to be a chi tonic. It has the capacity to build the energy reserves in the body while at the same time exhibiting several anti-stress properties. Astragalus Root enhances liver metabolism of endogenous and exogenous toxins. It shows a cardiotonic effect with the capacity of lowering blood pressure. It possesses marked antimicrobial properties especially against *Shigella spp.*, *Streptococcus haemolyticus*, and *Staphylococcus aureus*. It influences the kidney meridian and has been shown to improve urine flow and to be effective in urinary and bladder infections. If taken cumulatively, especially with Chinese *Ligustrum lucidum* berries, it shows marked anti-tumor properties.

Other plants which have been well studied for their adaptogenic effects include Holy Basil (*Ocimum sanctum*), Reishi mushroom (*Ganoderma lucidum*), and Gotu Kola (*Centella asiatica*). Other plants with less specific adaptogenic properties yet marked immune-stimulating properties and immunomodulating properties include species of Echinacea (*Echinacea angustfolia*, *Echinacea purpurea*, and *Echinacea pallida*).

Immune-Enhancing Properties of Echinacea

Echinacea is considered a nonspecific (adaptogenic) stimulant to the immune system, effecting a variety of viral and bacterial conditions influencing the secretory immune system. In this respect, Echinacea is recognized as a secretory immune stimulant influencing the mucous membranes, skin, and lymphatic system. The secretory immune system is recognized as the initial line of defense. *Echinacea spp.* contain a complex of different compounds responsible for their immune-enhancing effects. According to Christopher Hobbs in his monograph on Echinacea, much of the claims for Echinacea include stimulation of leukocytes, inhibition of the enzyme hyaluronidase, mild antibiotic activity, antiinflammatory activity, stimulation of the adrenal cortex, stimulation of the properdin/complement system, interferon-like activity, stimulation of phagocytosis (general cellular immunity), anti-viral activity, and increased production of fibroblasts.

During conceptual stages of viral infection, Echinacea can be very effective in frequent and large doses for preventing infection by inhibiting the enzyme hyaluronidase from breaking down the cell membrane and also by strengthening the cell membrane directly. Other secretory infections such as urinary tract infections, respiratory infections, sinus infections, ear infections, and tonsillitis, respond swiftly and convincingly to frequent and large doses of Echinacea at the onset of the infectious stage.

Adaptogenic and Immune-Enhancing Compounds

(See herbal dispensatory section for specific uses.)

Compounded Ginseng/Schizandra
Compounded Siberian Ginseng Tonic
Compounded Wild Ginseng
Compounded Gotu Kola
Compounded Rejuvenative Elixir
Compounded Smilax/Damiana
Compounded Vitamin C Elixir
Compounded Echinacea

Index

Y

Z

The Protocol Journal of Botanical Medicine

A concise quarterly publication devoted *exclusively* to therapeutic plant uses!

- An easy to use publication combining Western allopathic practices with Naturopathic, Ayurvedic, and Chinese practices.

- Therapeutic protocols with descriptions of contraindications, underlying chemistry and pharmacology, and complete citations from research conducted around the world.

- A peer-reviewed research publication offering current and thoroughly referenced material for both clinical and educational settings.

- Informative articles for naturopathic physicians, herbal educators, researchers, interested lay persons, as well as medical doctors and general practitioners.

Volume 1, No. 3

Disorders of Inflammation: benign prostatic hyperplasia, candidiasis, diabetes, kidney stones, peptic ulcer

Volume 1, No. 4

Women's Health: endometriosis, estrogen replacement therapy, mastitis, premenstrual syndrome cysts, uterine fibroids

Volume 2, No. 1

Mood, Memory, and Cerebral Vascular Disorders: affective mood disorders (depression), Alzheimer's disease, ADD/hyperactivity, tinnitus, Raynaud's Syndrome

Volume 2, No. 2

Disorders of the Eyes, Ears, and Throat: cataracts, glaucoma, otitis media, strep throat, sinus infection

— —

SUBSCRIPTION FORM

Call: (800) 466-5422

Or mail to:
The Protocol Journal
of Botanical Medicine
P.O. Box 108
Harvard, MA 01451

Domestic	Foreign
❏ 1 year (4 issues) – $96	❏ 1 year (4 issues) – $120US
❏ 2 years (8 issues) – $180	❏ 2 years (8 issues) – $220US

Name _____ Daytime phone _____

Address _____

City, State, Zip, Country _____

❏ Payment enclosed   ❏ Please bill me   ❏ VISA   ❏ MasterCard   ❏ American Express

Account number _____ Expiration date _____

Signature _____